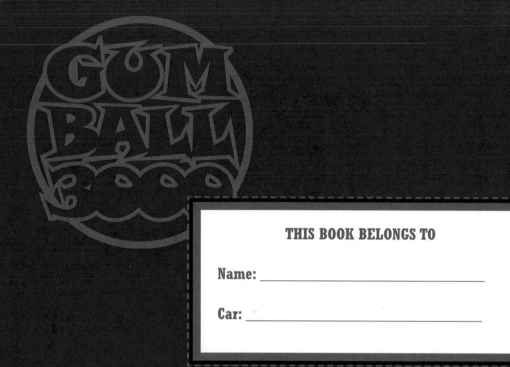

THIS BOOK BELONGS TO

Name: _____

Car: _____

Title: Gumball 3000
Sub Title: The Official Annual 2005
www.gumball3000.com

ISBN 0-9547226-1-2
EAN 9780954722616

Published by: Gumball 3000 Merchandise Limited
4 Lucerne Mews
London
W8 4ED
Great Britain

First Published: May 2005

Founders: Maximillion Cooper & Julie Brangstrup

Editor-In-Chief: Maximillion Cooper
Creative Directors: Camilla Lie Jenssen & Julia 'Joy' Martens

Produced and Edited by: Duncan Scholes
Art Direction: Camilla & Julia
Main Illustrator & Design: Matt Delahunt
Contributing Illustrators: Petter Wallenberg, Toma Jablon, Alex Eggert
Captain Gumball Artwork: Luc Janin
Main Writer: Tom Trinkle
Contributing Writers: Julia Martens, Nick Wyllys
Photo Editor: Nick Wyllys
Main Photographers: Fly, James McNaught, Fiona McLeod, Mike Dean, Nick Price
Contributing Photographers: Renton, Dan Anslow, Alex Roy, Ben Flames, Marc Melton, Duncan Ray
US Correspondent: Jarod DeAnda

National & International Distribution: Gardners Books Ltd, Bertrhams Books Ltd, THE (Total Home Entertainment)

Pass4Press PDFs created by FEBurman Ltd, London
Printed by: Imago Publishing Limited, Oxon

Cover Photos: Jonathan Bushell & Fly
Cover Artwork: Ben Flames & Mike Lawrence

Gumball 3000

"I'm the famous speaking 'Burt Reynolds' trophy that is awarded to all Gumballers that take part in the notorious rally. I have many magical powers that make Gumballers dreams and fantasy's come true. Some Gumballers have tried to use my powers to achieve their own corrupt wrong doings, and so now I am protected at all times by my own superhero, the legendary Captain Gumball. Anyone who abuses the powers of the Gumball BE WARNED – or else Captain Gumball will come to torment you for the rest of your life. Nothing can beat the power of the Gumball. Use the Gumball in the way it was intended and you will have happiness and adventure for the rest of your lives. And remember, Gumball is not just a rally – it's a way of life. Drive safely kids!"

Those of you lucky enough to own a 'Burt', you must remember to look after him. Many Gumballers have claimed they have lost or broken theirs over the years and have asked for a replacement. Unfortunately real 'Burt's' cannot be replaced, so treat him well and place him in a prominent position in your house and he will watch over your fortunes and make all your dreams and ambitions come true. If you place him in a box at the back of the garage your fortunes may well take a turn for the worse.

And if you ever need advice or counselling just ask Burt, he will be happy to advise you. On one rare occasion after a Gumballers fortunes took an unfortunate turn for the worse, Burt advised that as he had been treated so well, that if he sacrificed him all his problems would be resolved. Reluctantly the Gumballer took Burt's advice and he placed his 'Burt' Trophy awarded for participating in the 2000 rally on eBay. It sold for $9,000 and the Gumballer was happy again. The moral of the story is to make sure you look after your Burt, and your fellow Gumballers, and they will always look after you!

WANT TO IMPRESS YOUR FRIENDS? SIMPLY CUT OUT THE 'MAGICAL' GOLD GUMBALL 'BURT' TROPHY, STICK IT TO STIFF CARD AND PLACE ON YOUR MANTELPIECE. TELL ALL YOUR FRIENDS THAT YOU PARTICIPATED IN THE GUMBALL AND RECEIVED THIS COVETED TROPHY!

FANS!

AN INTRODUCTION

by Maximillion Cooper

Welcome back Gumball fans, to the Annual that brings you all the news and gossip from the famous 'Gumball 3000' rally.

To those of you that are new to the Gumball, in its simplest description the 'Gumball 3000' rally is a modern day version of the infamous 70s road trip movies – with a present-day cast that includes everyone from 'rock star to Royalty' to the avid car enthusiast. It has been described by Vogue as the most 'notorious and glamorous rally' that has ever existed, but the attraction of the Gumball transcends social barriers. The appeal is to the adventurer in all of us, regardless of status or wealth.

For those fortunate enough to participate in the event it has been a chance to forget everything and indulge in a passion for the machine that changed the world, the motorcar. For Gumball fans it has come to represent an aspiration and attitude expressive of living life to the full, with an 'air of rebellion' and a 'free spirit' that rarely exists elsewhere today, for many 'Gumball is not just a rally, it's a way of life!'

Now in its sixth year, in May 2004, 192 of the most amazing cars from around the world assembled in Paris to take part in another crazy adventure. For the next six days these cars drove across two Continents, from Paris down to Morocco, and back to Europe finishing in Cannes at the famous film festival.

The 2004 rally once again managed to combine grease, guts and glamour in equal measures, and this book enables us to share with you the highs and lows of the event from the comfort of your own home. With driver profiles, celebrity news, car reviews and competitions, there's enough fuel to feed any Gumballers needs until the next rally. So ladies and gentlemen, skater and king, pop star and princess, there you have it, sit back and fasten your seatbelts, you're in for one hell of a read…!

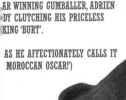

AR WINNING GUMBALLER, ADRIEN
DY CLUTCHING HIS PRICELESS
KING 'BURT'.

AS HE AFFECTIONATELY CALLS IT
MOROCCAN OSCAR!')

The Brains
MAXIMILLION COOPER

Welcome ladies and gentlemen to tonights show, our guests this evening are the 'brains and beauty' behind the famous and notorious 'Gumball 3000'. Let me first introduce its founder and creator, Maximillion Cooper...

LJ: So what is the Gumball 3000 Rally?
Max: Are you joking, you don't know what the Gumball is!

LJ: Of course I know, I saw it on the BBC with Ruby Wax a few years ago, and then on MTV with Johnny Knoxville at the wheel, but tell me, when and why did you start it?
Max: Well, I started Gumball six years ago in my initial quest to create something really stylish in the motoring world.

For the past 11 years I've been racing cars on and off, and I'd grown up lovin' anything with wheels, from skateboarding to BMX and motocross; then I spent a few years in London designing at St. Martins College, hanging out with a really creative and influential crowd. Whilst I loved racing cars I found the whole industry pretty boring because it's become so corporate, especially Formula

MAX BY HIS MORGAN AERO 8 IN CASABLANCA (2004)

One, so I had the idea to start my own Formula One team, a real rock 'n' roll race team.

LJ: That's a pretty big ambition to achieve, so how did you go about it?
Max: Back in 1998 I tried to buy the Tyrrell F1 team but got outbid by British American Tobacco, and ironically at the time I was still in my final year of a Law degree and I

actually had no money, but I had gained the support of a few backers willing to support my dream. So when the Tyrrell bid didn't succeed I needed another

KARTA HANGING OUT OF MAX'S BENTLEY ARNAGE RED LABEL (2000)

approach to the vision and realised that if I got all my friends together I'd have more of a chance of achieving it. So with that in mind, I decided to invite them on my own week long magical mystery tour and take it from there. That was back in 1999 and that was the first Gumball!

LJ: Wow, that was quite a master plan. Gumball's grown somewhat since then, the plan seems to be working.
Max: Yeah, well I had the bigger vision behind it all, in that I wanted to create an entity or brand that

Luc Janin

1999

1999 was Gumball 3000's founding year. Maximillion Cooper invited 50 of his most eccentric friends to take part in a 6 day 3000 mile drive around Europe, partying each night. The event kicked off with a party at the Bluebird Club attended by London's A-list including Kate Moss, Billy Zane, Guy Ritchie, Chris Eubank, Dannii Minogue and Monica Lewinski.

Sir Terence Conran dropped the chequered flag and 55 cars set off from London to Rimini and back, covering 6 countries, 2 Principalities, 5 Grand prix circuits and 3000 miles

Vivienne Westwood, YMC, Diesel, Jitrois, Duffer of St George and Anthony Price create Gumball driving suits for the participants. Gumball signs a sponsorship deal with Italian fashion giants Diesel who provide luggage for everyone.

Chris Eubank rolls in 12 hours behind the rest of the pack in his Peterbuilt truck and Dannii Minogue completes the drive in her Porsche Boxter. Jason Priestley (Beverly Hill's 90210) 150 mph was forgiven for an autograph!

LONDON
CHATEAU D'ESCLIMONT
HOCKENHEIM GRAND PRIX CIRCUIT
SCHLOSS AMBRAS
LE MANS
PARIS
MAS DU CLOS
MONACO
RIMINI
MODENA FERRARI FACTORY

CHRIS EUBANK

JASON PRIESTLEY

would appeal to all my friends, from skateboarders to bank bosses. And there are no other brands like it, how often is a skateboarder and a banker into the same thing, and yet both are proud to have a 'Gumball' sticker on either their skateboard deck or flash car. Gumball has managed to

MAX'S JAMES BOND LOTUS ESPRIT AT MI6 (1999)

combine all the cool ingredients of the music, fashion, film, motoring and 'street' cultures into one.

LJ: So what I want to know is what is it about the Gumball that has made it such a phenomenon?
Max: The Gumball rally itself is just insane, for one week your life goes into Gumball mode, it's a full on balls out extraordinary event, there's nothing else like it on this planet !

LJ: You make it sound exhausting, I thought Gumball was just one party

after the next with famous bands and DJs playing?
Max: Yes, there are parties each night, but Gumball is so much more than just a party. Its probably the biggest endurance that you will ever experience.

LJ: That doesn't sound easy?
Max: No one said it was easy. If Batman took a vacation, this is the sort of trip that he'd take, because it's not for the weak.

LJ: So if it's that hard why would I want to do the Gumball?
Max: Maybe you wouldn't. But if you are up for having an adventure then there's none better. After doing the Gumball you'll experience life in a new way, it's an education as much as an adventure, you learn a lot about yourself, push yourself beyond your normal limits and really live life to the max!

LJ: And you stay in nice

hotels, right?
Max: Yeah sure, the hotels we stay in are all 5-star, everything on the route adds to the experience. Past checkpoints have included everything from the Barcelona 'Grand Prix' and Real Madrid's football stadium, to famous houses like Elvis Presley's Graceland and the 'Playboy Mansion', but the Gumball could never be described as being a straight forward 5-star week. I like to keep everything as a surprise for all the participants, and so one night we may stay in the most amazing

MAX PRESENTING AWARDS IN CANNES (2004)

2000

The second Gumball Rally. May 2000. 85 cars, 3 motorbikes, 7 countries, 6 days 3000 miles. The flag dropped at Marble Arch, and drivers are directed to Stansted Airport where two Russian Cargo planes airlift everyone to Spain. The rally attracts several entrants from the music industry, with Goldie taking part in an Aston Martin V8 with Cass from Skunk Anansie, along with Placebo in an Aston Martin Lagonda, the Happy Mondays in a Jag and soul diva Kym Mazelle being chauffeur driven in a BMW.

Channel 4 show the rally as a 30 minute Gumball Special and Gumball signs a license deal to produce Gumball 3000 Rally Top Trumps playing cards.

ASTON MARTIN V8

Great Train Robber Bruce Reynolds enters in a Bentley claiming the Gumball to be ' the greatest adventure left'! Everyone receives specially commissioned bronze heads of Cannonball legend Burt Reynolds.

"I DO?"

Another Gumball first takes place when 'it-girl' Tara Palmer-Tomkinson marries a film director she has only just met on the rally aboard the ferry crossing from Hamburg to Harwich.

LOTUS FACTORY
HAMBURG
LONDON
NURBURGRING GP CIRCUIT
SCHLOSS BUHLERHOHE
BILBAO
MILANO
CANNES
GUMBALL YACHT
PRIVATE AIRPORT
IN SPAIN

Châteaux, and the next night you could be in a tent. Afterwards you'll think, wow, did I just do all that in one week. It's actually such an experience that it's genuinely too much to comprehend during the event, it's days, weeks and months afterwards that you truly realise what you did that week. Insane!

AC COBRA "WHICH WAY TO LITHUANIA?" (2001)

LJ: We haven't mentioned the cars, there's an obscene amount of Ferraris, Lambos and other supercars, it seems like there's a lot of horsepower on the Gumball, is it a race?

Max: Are you trying to catch me out here? If Gumball was a race on public roads that would be illegal, and I'd probably be in jail by now. It's not like you could turn up into any city and park over 100 cars on display for 12 hours unnoticed, cause a huge disturbance, and then cruise on out of town without the help and support of the local police and sometimes even the

Government. The Gumball isn't the illegal race that sometimes the media, fans and even participants would like it to be. That doesn't mean to say that 'some' participants don't have their own brush with the law, but as long as we keep it safe people do generally get away with things that normally would have them locked up. Gumball is for fun, it's an amazing spectacle, the police and local people generally love it. It's not everyday an event like the Gumball comes to town.

THE HOSTS WITH THE MOST (2004)

LJ: What is it about the Gumball that makes it so appealing?

Max: Driving down the highway, through towns and villages, with over 100 other amazing vehicles all on the same trip, it's the biggest blast! Many of the experiences are things that even when they are happening you think to yourself, this could never happen again. It's a real once in a life time experience.

LJ: So what's planned for 2005?

Max: The route in 2005 is just off the scale, after staring at the 'war map' on the wall in the HQ, I've come up with a 3000 mile route that has everything the Gumball needs. It's got amazing cities, travels through 13 countries, incorporates sections of both the legendary Italian 'Mille

MAX USES A PORSCHE TURBO FROM NY TO LA (2002)

Miglia' and 'Targa Florio' Sicilian historic motor races and ends at the famous Monaco Grand Prix.

LJ: When and where will that start be?

Max: The dates are set for the rally to finish at the Monaco Grand Prix, so the start in London will be the Saturday prior to the Monaco GP. All cars will go on display on Friday 13th May, and the start flag will drop on the Sunday evening.

LJ: And the route?

Max: Without giving too much away, after leaving England key check points include the stunning

2001

The third rally, April 2001. 106 Cars, 13 Countries, 6 days, 3000 miles. From London to Russia and back again. Despite the fear of car jacking and lawlessness in Eastern Europe everyone survives the experience unscathed. The first leg from Hyde Park Corner in London, through Germany, Poland and onto Lithuania takes many drivers more than 30 hours non-stop!

JOHNNY KNOXVILLE

F1 World Champion Damon Hill is in pole position for the off and claims that he's as proud of this pole as I am of any of the 201 scored in Formula One".

BBC1 send Ruby Wax on the rally for a TV Documentary, capturing the event in front of an audience of ten's of millions. MTV becomes media partners and enter a crew of 12 people to follow the antics of Johnny Knoxville and the rest of the Jackass' for a special hour-long Gumball Jackass episode. The MTV Gumball show is the highest viewed show on MTV of the year. The www.gumball 3000.com becomes the most searched website on yahoo and Goggle search engines!

RUBY WAX

cities of Prague, Vienna, Budapest, and Dubrovnik in Croatia, before lapping Sicily in true 'Targa Florio' style and then following the historic route of the famous 'Millie Miglia' up the Italian coast to Rome before crossing the finish line in Monte Carlo's Casino Square!

MAX'S LAMBORGHINI MURCIELAGO IN SAN FRAN (2003)

LJ: And any parties?
Max: Yes of course, apart from the parties for participants we're also organising huge public music concerts in the 4 main cities en route. London will host the first concert the night before the start. Maybe this year we'll actually get Jay Kay on the trip and get Jamiroquai to play live at the end. Who knows? If you are listening Jay it's about time you took that Enzo for a little drive!

LJ: Mentioning Jay Kay, what about other celebrities?
Max: Yeah over the years we've had everyone from Johnny Knoxville and the rest of the Jackass guys, to

popstars and bands like Dannii Minogue, 'Placebo' and 'The Happy Mondays', DJs Goldie and Norman Jay, loads of actors, including Jason Priestley and Adrien Brody, the 'Oscar' winning star of 'The Pianist', ex-F1 world champion Damon Hill, ex-Boxing world champion Chris Eubank, skateboard legends Tony Hawk and Bucky Lasek, Motocross legends Carey Hart and Travis Pastrana and even horse racing champion jockey Richard Dunwoody. What a line up! With that sort of pedigree we'll have one or two interesting faces in 2005, that's for sure!

MAX AND JULIE - LOVE AT 200MPH (2001)

LJ: What car will you be driving?
Max: I'd love to drive the new Ford GT if I get one in time. And if I thought a Porsche 917 or Ferrari P4 would do the trip I'd take either of those (if I owned them)!

LJ: Cool cars. This all sounds like a pretty big operation. Do you run

this all on your own?
Max: Yeah right! That's like when people ask me 'what do I do the rest of the year?' Gumball is now quite an Empire, we've got companies that run everything from the rally, to our own clothing label 'G3K', to making movies, publishing books, to looking after all the license and merchandise deals. It's a huge full

ALWAYS 007 (2004)

time operation, and we've now got offices all around the world!

LJ: You say "we've", who are you referring to?
Max: Oh, that's my wife, Julie, she runs the companies with me!

LJ: Does she do the rally to?
Max: Yeah, always, and she drives real hard too!

LJ: She sounds cool, and clever too, do you mind if I ask her a few questions?
Max: Please do. She's a real Danish Viking though, so be warned!

STARS'N'STRIPES 'VETTE'

The fourth rally, April 2002 in the United States, New York to LA, finishing at the Playboy Mansion. 175 Cars, 3 Motorbikes, 13 States, 6 days, 3000 miles!

Sony Playstation releases a Gumball 3000 PS2 game and Gumball gets featured in over 10,000 magazines around the world.

After being pulled over by police, a solution to appease the cops is to give them a ride in the car. Team Texas records on film the speedometer of their RUF Porsche at 206mph with a cop in the passenger seat. All he says is 'sweet. That's something to tell the grandkids about!'

Donna Karen sponsors the event with DKNY Jeans label, making a race jacket for all participants. Post the 9/11 devastation Gumball raises awareness for the Twin Towers Foundation and auction's off a place on the rally on Ebay for the fund.

Four playmates of the Year enter the Rally in a new Mini Cooper. Hugh Hefner and Bunny's present the awards at the legendary Playboy Mansion. Gumball heaven!

2002

BUNNIES

NEW YORK
WASHINGTON DC
LAS VEGAS   GRAND CANYON   NASHVILLE
LA   SANTA FE
PLAYBOY   GRACELAND
MANSION   CADILLAC   ELVIS' HOUSE
               RANCH   DALLAS

The Beauty
JULIE BRANGSTRUP

LJ: Welcome ladies and gentlemen to the other half of 'Team Gumball', Julie Brangstrup (applause and whistles). So Julie, you're the brains and the beauty behind the scenes. This is not a bad thing you've created, you must be happy?

Julie: Hi Lay, it's a pleasure to meet you. Gumball is definately an exciting company to run, even if, when I met Max back in 2000, I thought it was the most disorganised, craziest thing I'd ever seen!

LJ: So you only met Max a few years ago. So what happened, you fell in love and then started to work with each other, that's pretty hardcore?

Julie: I guess what really happened is that I'd come from working in the financial world, and Max from the 'arts' world, and so naturally our working relationship works very well. I keep ontop of the business, so that Max can keep being creative.

LJ: And so whats your goal with the Gumball?

Julie: A couple of years back my Aunt won 'Business Woman of the Year' Award, and I'd like to think that one day, if things keep progressing the way they are that I might follow in her footsteps.

LJ: Have you got any specific ideas for the future?

Julie: Yes, one of the areas I'm concentrating on is to open up a chain of boutique Gumball stores and hotels, and I'm also working towards setting up a Gumball hedgefund. The concept already has the support of many leading financial figureheads from around the world, many of them participate in the Gumball. We'll be announcing our full stragergy in the coming months.

LJ: Wow, sounds exciting. I also heard that you've had time to have two children. Hows that possible?

Julie: Yes, we've got two beautiful daughters, Lotus and Jagger. They come everywhere with us, and have even driven the past two Gumball 'recce's', meeting the Mayors of each city. Gumball's a very family event you see!!!

LJ: Cool names? What do they get up to?

Julie: Right now they are only 2 1/2 and 1, but who knows, we may end up with a couple of future F1 champions on our hands?

LJ: I'm sure they are very proud of their parents. Anyway folks, thats all we've got time for tonight. I'd like to thank tonights guests, Maximillion Cooper & his beautiful wife Julie Brangstrup.

MMC 11

SHE'S A DANISH VIKING - BE WARNED!!!

Timeline:

RENO
LAS VEGAS
SAN FRANCISCO
WHITE SANDS
TUCSON
NEW ORLEANS
SAN ANTONIO
MIAMI

2003

The fifth annual rally from San Francisco to Miami. May 2003. 145 cars, 9 states, 6 Days 3000 miles!

Jackass moviestar Ryan Dunn builds his BMW 318 for the rally with 600bhp under the hood. The engine blows up days before the start and he ends up renting a Hertz Cadillac DeVille in San Francisco. The Koenigsegg CC supercar allegedly reaches 242mph. Freestyle MX legend Carey Hart jumps over the cars Evil Knievel style in Las Vegas.

Gumball 3000 'The Movie' has its global premiere at London's Leicester Square Odeon. Paparazzi and over 5000 Gumball fans take over central London. Porn star legend Ron Jeremy and model Jodie Marsh are among the many celebs at the premiere.

Royal Elastic's create a Gumball driving boot and Top Trumps release Gumball Supercars. Top Gear features supermodel Jodie Kidd to discuss the Gumball. She denies any speed antics.

MTV's notorious Cuban Brothers break dance naked at the pre-rally party to the shock of the clubowner.

KOENIGSEGG CC

RYAN DUNN

Our story begins in *PARIS*

Welcome to the 6th annual Gumball 3000 Rally. I hope you had a pleasant trip to Paris.

As for the next 6 days.... life is going to be an adventure!

"The routecard made me do it.."

Over the next few days the Gumballers were told where to eat sleep and drive via several routecards that directed them to the next party, hotel, or checkpoint.

MAXIMILLION WAVES THE "TRICOLOR"

Nick Price

**FOUR SEASONS
GEORGE V HOTEL
PARIS, FRANCE
4 MAY 2004**

Overnight all vehicles will be scrutineered, numbered and branded in the 'Gumball livery' ready to go!

Learn to say: "Salut mon nom est Burt, je suis riche et conduit un Ferrari, aimeriez-vous avoir une boisson avec moi?" ("Hi my name is Burt, I'm rich and drive a Ferrari, would you like to have a drink with me?")

When 192 supercars started parking up outside the Eiffel Tower, the crowds and press began to gather...

THE CARS LINE UP AROUND THE TROCADERO FOR THE START OF THE RALLY

Kim Schmitz

* 001 Peterbilt truck and Bentley Arnage T *002 Mercedes ML *003 Range Rover *004 Lamborghini Murcielago *005 Ferrari 360 Spid H2 *014 Mercedes Benz SL55 *015 Porsche Cayenne GT700 Gemballa *016 Bentley Arnage *017 Ferrari Enzo *018 Mini *019 Porsc Porsche Cayenne S *028 Lamborghini Murcielago *029 Hummer H2 *030 Ferrari 360 *031 Mercedes CLK320 *032 Ferrari Ch 1.8T *038 BMW 645 cab *039 BMW CSL *042 Maserati Spider E *043 Aston Martin DB7 *044 Mercedes SL500 *046 D Bentley Continental GT *053 Porsche GT2 *054 Ford 4x4 Van V10 *055 Porsche Cabriolet *056 Nissan Skyline 33GT- Porsche 911 966 *063 Lamborghini Murcielago *064 Porsche 911 Turbo *065 BMW M3 *066 BMW M3 AC Schnitz Turbo *073 Porsche 996 Turbo *074 Porsche Techart Turbo *075 Noble M12 GTO3R *076 Porsche 996 *077 C 993 Turbo *083 Porsche 996 GT3 RS *084 Peugeot 406 Coupe *085 Lotus Elise *086 Hummer H2 *087 911 Turbo *092 Mercedes SL55 *093 Ferrari 355 GTS *094 Porsche GT3 *095 Noble M12 GTO 3R * *100 Chevrolet SSR *101 Jaguar E-type *102 Ferrari 550 Maranello *103 Mercedes SL55 *104 Ran Carrera 2 *109 Porsche RUF 911 *110 Porsche Cayenne Turbo *111 Audi RS6 *112 Citroen 2CV Mercedes CL55 AMG *117 Ferrari 360 Spider *118 Porsche 928 GTS *119 Caterham 7 Sup Vantage *123 BMW X3 *124 Porsche 911 Speedster *125 Porsche 911 Targa *126 Fe *129 Ferrari Modena 360 * 130 Aston Martin Virage 6.3 *131 BMW M3 *132 B *136 Porsche 966 Turbo * 138 London Taxi *139 Hummer H2 *140 Bentle Porsche 911 C2 *143 Aston Martin DB7 Vantage *144 BMW M5 *145 Po AMG SL55 *148 Dodge Viper SRT-10 *149 Ferrari 360 Spider * 150 Evo 8 * 152 Bentley Continental R * 153 Police Car * 154 BM SL55 * 156 Limousine Lincoln Town Car * 157 Porsche Nissan 350C * 160 BMW 8 Series * 161 Saleen S Lamborghini Gallardo * 164 Mercedes SL55 Mercedes E320 * 167 AIYA – Winnebego 200 VW Beetle * 168-191 Crew cars and support vehicles

192 CARS
768,000 BHP
$28,800,000 WORTH OF MACHINERY
TAKE YOUR PICK!!!

The Grid

*007 Morgan Aero 8 *008 BMW X5 *009 Bentley Continental GT *010 Maserati Spider *011 Porsche Cayenne *012 Hummer
es SL500 *021 Porsche 996 Cab 4S *023 Mercedes C55 AMG *024 Ferrari Enzo *025 Audi RS6 *026 BMW M3 *027
Ferrari 360 Modena *034 Ferrari 360 Spider *035 Ferrari 360 Spider *036 Porsche Techart Turbo *037 VW Golf
Mercedes ML400 *048 BMW M3 *049 Ferrari 360 Modena *050 Ferrari 575M F1 *051 BMW M3 * 052
*058 Ferrari 360 Spider *059 Porsche GT3 *060 Ford Mustang GT500E *061 Porsche 911 * 062
Turbo *069 Mini Cooper *070 Porsche 996 Turbo *071 Ferrari Modena Cabrio *072 Porsche
all S *078 Ferrari 575 *079 Volvo V70R *081 Aston Martin DB7 Vantage *082 Porsche
MG *088 Ferrari 360 *089 Mercedes CL5 *090 Porsche Boxter *091 Porsche
MW 330 Sport Diesel *098 Ferrari 360 *099 Subaru Impreza WRX STI
*105 Chrysler Crossfire *106 Lotus Elise 135 Sport *107 Porsche
*114 Mustang Shelby GT350 *115 Mercedes CL500 *116
*121 Mercedes E55 AMG *122 Aston Martin DB7
27 Bentley Continental GT *128 TVR Tuscan
745 Li *134 Porsche 911 Carrera 4
141 Ferrari 360 Spider *142
355 *147 Mercedes
151 Mitsubishi
rcedes

THE KING'S MEN KEEP A WATCHFUL EYE!!

Frederike Helwig

2004 Ferrari Enzo

Named after the godfather of Ferrari himself, the Enzo is the fastest road car ever built by the company, and can achieve 0-60mph in 3.75 seconds. It is as close as a member of the public can get to driving the Ferrari piloted to three Formula One World Championships by Michael Schumacher, who incidentally was involved in the development of the Enzo. Among the top-flight features are a carbon fibre chassis and carbon ceramic disc brakes as well as aerodynamic fins and a rear spoiler that activate at high speeds. Expensive, rare (only 349 have been made), aggressively styled and unbelievably fast – the Enzo couldn't be classified as anything else but a 'supercar'.

"KEEP BACK KIDS!"

Mark Kershaw

PERFORMANCE

Max speed:	218 mph
0-60:	3.7 sec
Max power:	650 bhp
Miles per gallon:	13 mpg
Engine capacity:	5998 cc
Cost when new:	$800,000
Total produced:	349

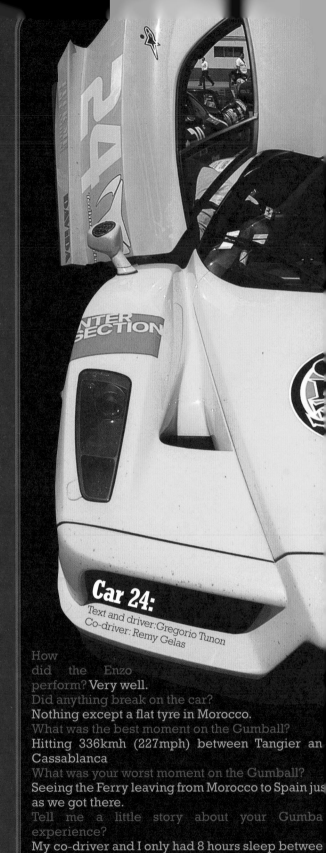

Car 24:
Text and driver: Gregorio Tunon
Co-driver: Remy Gelas

How did the Enzo perform? **Very well.**
Did anything break on the car?
Nothing except a flat tyre in Morocco.
What was the best moment on the Gumball?
Hitting 336kmh (227mph) between Tangier an Cassablanca
What was your worst moment on the Gumball?
Seeing the Ferry leaving from Morocco to Spain jus as we got there.
Tell me a little story about your Gumba experience?
My co-driver and I only had 8 hours sleep betwee Paris and Cannes which caused my co-driver t start hallucinating. He was seeing yellow sheep b the side of the road and thought that there wa someone climbing the ladder of a tanker lorr

whilst on the motorway. We got a puncture in Morocco so we could not go fast afterwards until we replaced it as we only had tyre weld to fix the tyre with. We had a support car following us during the rally until the driver went mad and drove to Madrid instead of Barcelona after missing the ferry in Nador. It carried spare parts and our luggage as there is no room in the Enzo for anything. We had been told by everyone to be careful of the Spanish Police because they were looking for us and would come down hard on us. We were going at 300kmh (188mph) and came round a corner to find two police cars. They were talking to each other and neither of them even turned their heads as we screamed past.

Marks out of 10 for your cars performance? 10.

"FOLLOW THAT MINI!"

FERRARI HISTORY

Enzo Ferrari first built his own racing car, the 125C Sport, in 1947 and achieved immediate success on the circuit. Since then, the company based in Maranello, Italy has gained a reputation for building some of the finest cars in the world, often making versions of its race cars for use on the road. The 1950s was a golden era for Ferrari racing when the team won four Formula One world driver's championship titles. Further success came in the 1970s with the introduction of a new 180 degree V12 engine that helped Ferrari secure three more Formula One driver's championships. The same engine was used in Ferrari road cars such as the Testarossa until 1996. The latest run of triumphs has come courtesy of the invincible Michael Schumacher with his record of four consecutive world driver's championships beginning in 2000. Ferrari has also won the Formula One constructor's championship 13 times, which is the record and further confirmation, if any was needed, of the company's prime place in motoring history.

"FOLLOW THAT MINI!"

"BELLISSIMO!"

SUPER CARS

Gumball Factor: ★ ★ ★ ★ ★

Car 04:

Text and driver: Aidan Butler
Co-driver: Russell Sealey

2004 LAMBORGHINI MURCIELAGO

James Mc Naught

With a 6.2-litre V12 engine that can take it from 0-60mph in 3.8 seconds, the Murcielago is comparable in performance to the Ferrari Enzo, placing it firmly at the top end of the supercar bracket. This Lambo is also packed with fascinating design features such as bodywork mainly composed of carbon fibre panels, the company's renowned scissor doors that open upwards rather than outwards and 18-inch wheels that are designed to suck air in to help cool the enormous disc brakes. In fact, the extra stopping power is vital, especially when this raging bull sees the red at the top end of the rev counter!

How did it perform?

Brilliantly! At 4am, after a 30 hour drive to Marbella the whole car felt like dying. In the morning when it had cooled down, it felt fantastic again.

What was your top speed? 203 mph

Did anything break on the car?

Yes. The electric windows stopped working. At one point, only the passenger window would open a little bit so I would end up covering my sleeping co-driver in cigarette ash.

What was the best moment on the Gumball?

Meeting my fiancee and driving in Morocco.

What was your worst moment on the Gumball?

Getting arrested on the second day of the Gumball. Me and the red Enzo were ahead of a pack of 60 cars and we were pulled by the Gendarme so I hid my radar detector. They had thought it was my air freshener and seeing a detector nowhere they said we could go. We decided to wait for 5 minutes for another car to show by which time the police had decided to pull over all the Gumballers because someone had used a radar jammer so they didn't let us leave. The driver of the Red Enzo and I looked at each other and we said to each other "Shall we do a runner..... yup...ok.. lets do it..!" We burnt off being chased by a French Gendarme on foot frantically blowing his whistle. We drove without incident for 2 hours before being pulled again by 3 Police Motorcycles. We had to drive to the station where we proceeded to be told "You don't get rights in France, you're English!" After hours of negotiation, (the Enzo driver being my solicitor and taking the piss out of the officers boots) and cutting the wires to the radar detector, they let us go... and all through this my co-driver was asleep in the passenger seat.

Marks out of 10 for your cars performance? 9.

'Murcielago' means bat in Spanish and it was also the name of a famous Spanish bull in the late 19th century who resisted the sword of the best matador in Barcelona to live on and father a line of exceptional fighting bulls. It's an appropriate name for the latest supercar from a company whose logo depicts a raging bull. Designed by Luc Donkerwolke, the Murcielago does not have the OTT styling of the Countach and it is easier to drive than its immediate predecessor, the Diablo.

MORE GADGETS THAN JAMES BOND

Renton

WHICH WAY DID THE SUPERMODEL GO?

Scott Andrew

Car 63:

Text and driver: Ian Griffin
Co-driver: Simon Hewetson
How did it perform?
Great! We had 640bhp!
What was your top speed? 220 mph
Did anything break on the car?
No. The car has a sensor in the air boxes that controls the engine management system. In Cannes, because of the humidity or something like that, the computer kept revving the engine. We felt really embarrassed as everyone thought that we were showing off.
What was the best moment on the Gumball?
Chasing the Red Enzo in France and arriving in Cassablanca 3/4 hour before anyone else.
What was your worst moment on the Gumball?
Undertaking a Gumballer around a corner who was doing 145mph. I could see my line perfectly but the Gumballer didn't see us and turned in. I ended up drifting the car at 200mph and so nearly hit the arm co. It was scary and calmed us all down a bit. My co-driver refused to drive with me any further at that point.
Tell me a little story about your Gumball experience?
I have a TV and DVD player fitted to the car. My co-driver was watching The Office on it. We were speeding round a corner and I shouted to him to see if it was clear. He replied "Where's the pause button?".
Marks out of 10 for your cars performance? 10

GUMBALL3000.COM

G52 BXF

PERFORMANCE

Max speed:	205 mph
0-60:	3.6 sec
Max power:	580 bhp
Miles per gallon:	11 mpg
Engine capacity:	6192 cc
Cost when new:	$195,000
Total produced:	n/a

FLY

SUPER CARS
Gumball Factor: ★★★★★

PERFORMANCE

Max speed:	186 mph
0-60:	4.1 sec
power:	420 bhp
per gallon:	n/a
capacity:	3586 cc
	$235.00
	n/a

Ben Raines

2004 FERRARI 360 CHALLENGE STRADALE

IF I STAND HERE LONG ENOUGH - WILL IT BE MINE?

Renton

KEVLAR HEAVEN

Like the GTO, the 275 and the F40, the 360 Challenge Stradale is another Ferrari road car that was born on the racetrack. The legendary Italian manufacturer has fitted it with the minimum of equipment to make it legal to drive on the street. This means the Stradale has raw interior with very little concession to comfort, with bare carbon fibre panels and no carpet, sound-deadening, or for that matter sound system. However, the sheer performance of this rare Ferrari (only a few hundred were made) more than makes up for the lack of an in-car entertainment system. The 3.6-litre V8 engine can produce 425bhp and propels the lightweight aluminium car to breathtaking speeds, while the titanium coil springs that provide the suspension are set stiff and low for responsive handling. The Stradale produces an amazing noise, in part thanks to an exhaust system that bypasses the muffler when the car is driven fast, setting the incredibly loud engine sounds free at high speed.

BORN FOR THE RACE TRACK

NOT JUST ANOTHER RED FERRARI!

Dan Aseltine

FERRARI LOGO HISTORY

Ferrari's Cavallino Rampante (prancing horse) logo was originally used by Count Francesco Barraca, a legendary pilot in the Italian air force in World War One who won 34 duels and numerous team victories before being shot down. In 1923, Barraca's mother Countess Paolina granted Enzo Ferrari permission to use the horse logo after seeing him win a race in Ravenna. He first used it in 1932 on the Scuderia Ferrari team racing cars built by Alfa Romeo but since then it has become the famous insignia of his own range of exceptional cars. Enzo added the yellow background to the logo because it was the symbolic colour of his town Modena.

Nick Price

SUPER CARS

Gumball Factor: ★★★★☆

TRACTORS & LAMBORGHINIS
THE HISTORY OF THE BULL

By the 1960s Ferrucio Lamborghini had built up a successful business manufacturing tractors and other agricultural machinery. Among other sports cars, he owned several Ferraris and when the clutch failed on one of them he took it back to the factory. Lamborghini was enraged when Enzo Ferrari refused to meet him and answer his complaints, so he returned home and had a go at fixing the car himself. Surprised by the simplicity of the repair, Lamborghini began building his own road-going cars using modified Fiat parts and bearing the same charging bull insignia found on his tractors (inspired by his interest in bullfighting and his star sign, Taurus). When Lamborghini set up his state-of-the-art factory in Sant'Agata with the intention of bettering Ferrari based in nearby Maranello, Enzo sneered, "What does a tractor maker know about super cars? Go back to your farm and leave the super cars to me." Since unveiling his first production car, the 350 GT, in 1964, Lamborghini has produced a string of unforgettable super cars all with names relating to bullfighting including the Miura (1966), the Countach (1974), the Diablo (1990) and, of course, the Gallardo and the Murcielago.

POLIZIA GALLARDO

Lamborghini has donated a Gallardo supercar to an unlikely recipient – the Rome state police! Like all police cars it is fitted with flashing lights, a siren and a radio but it is used specifically for fast emergency response on the Salerno–Reggio–Calerna highway and the transportation of medical equipment for emergencies and blood and organs for transplant.

SPOT THE GUMBALL!!

Car163: Text and driver: Robin Johnson, co-driver: Marcus Lund

How did it perform?
Sweetly, only overtaken once and that was by the yellow ENZO!
Did anything break on the car?
Only a 1970's Peugeot 304 when I hit it!
What was the best moment on the Gumball?
Taking the Piss out of Andy Mill's dodgy tracksuits.
What was your worst moment on the Gumball?
Forced to miss the grand Prix in Barcelona by the police.
Any other problems with the police?
Where do I start? Day 1, after Mas Du Clos; Casually driving along at 150 mph – I spotted a guy with a camera. I thought he was a gumball fan with a video so I accelerated up to about 170mph (275 kmph) – unfortunately it was the law. Fortunately these were 'nice' French policeman. They booked me for doing 221kmph, because if you drive faster than 222 kmph then they have to impound your car. A small matter of 750 euros and they took my license away too.
Day 2 - Near Bordeaux; Pulled together with another 10 cars including Kev in his Red Enzo and lush girlfriend, Nick in his M3 sporting a rather spectacular floppy hat, Aiden and Russ in the Murcielago and other completely 'innocent' gumballers. Apparently we all had radar detectors! What!
We were asked to wait ten minutes but after an hour or so we were getting angry. Those that hadn't had their licenses or passports held were encouraged to 'get the f*** out of Dodge' by the rest of us. So Kev and Aiden decided to break for the Spanish border. You can just imagine the scene. Two of the loudest and most spectacular cars in the rally trying to sneak out of the car park complex. It was as subtle as a Spitfire in fly past mode at 50 feet. Guess what! They were spotted... and rumour has it that they had their trousers pulled down good and proper by more French plod just before the border. Bad luck guys! For the rest, some radar detectors were found followed by swift 750 euro kicks in the nuts.
Marks out of 10 for your cars performance?

Nick Price

9.

Car150: Text and driver: Rory Maton, Co-driver: Shaun Neumann

How did it perform? Awesome!

Did anything break on the car? No.

What was the best moment on the Gumball? So many to choose from!

What was your worst moment on the Gumball? Watching other Gumballers crash.

A little story about your Gumball experience? The Gumball was madness this year. I bought the car specially for this Gumball and picked it up from the factory in Italy a week before the start in Paris. I already had 4 tickets before the Gumball started, got 6 during the rally and managed to get 1 afterwards!

Marks out of 10 for your cars performance? Definately a 10.

James Mc Naught

"IS THAT THE BATMOBILE???"

2004 Lamborghini Gallardo

This Lambo is cheaper than the Murcielago but on the surface it is hard to tell them apart. The key to spotting the difference is the slightly chunkier appearance of the Gallardo and its headlamp housings which are slender shapes compared to the fatter shaped housings on the Murcielago. Although not as awesomely powerful as its bigger brother, the Gallardo still packs a considerable punch with a five-litre V10 engine that produces 500bhp. The car's manual six-speed gearbox can be switched to the clutchless E-Gear mode in which gears are changed electronically with the same steering-column-mounted paddle shifters used by Ferrari. The Gallardo does not have the spectacular scissor doors of other Lamborghinis and the influence of the company's German owners Audi is evident, especially on the interior. However, its unmistakable roar confirms this car still has an Italian soul.

PERFORMANCE

Max speed:	192 mph
0-60:	4.2 sec
Max power:	493 bhp
Miles per gallon:	n/a
Engine capacity:	4961 cc
Cost when new:	$165,000
Total produced:	n/a

SUPER CARS

Famous Gumballer - Shane 'The Legend' Slevin

French celebrity couple David and Cathy Guetta hosted the pre-rally party in their neo-'70s decor nightclub 'La Suite', the mecca of the Parisian fashion world!

Famous at La Suite

Famous Pulp Fiction Film Star Tim Roth

Famous Soul Diva Kym Mazelle

Famous Playboy Playmate Shanna Moakler with famous Playmate friends getting groovy

Above: Famous Oscar Winner Adrien Brody with famous skateboard legends Tony Hawk and Bucky Lasek

Left: Famous Supermodel Jodie Kidd

F**K ME

ande

5 Mai 2004, Paris

Cathy and David Guetta

King & Queen of Paris Nightlife

David is famed for his upbeat combination of contagious house DJ styles and came to prominence in Ibiza through his own 'F**k Me, I'm Famous' parties at Pasha!

Together they own a strip club, a sell-out night in Ibiza, an exclusive nightclub in France and a hit single all over the world. His CD "F**k Me I'm Famous: Dj Mix Ibiza", that contains his remix of David Bowie's "Heroes" has become a club classic!

What's your daily ride? Cab.
Favorite clothing brand? Just a sexy, worn in t-shirt.
What's you favorite magazine? Numero.
What kind of party did you host in La Suite? Famous, fashion, and happy people.
What was the atmosphere of this group of people who were about to lap a 3000 mile circuit around Europe and Africa? People were happy to be participating and happy to be partying.
Did you catch any crazy stories or gossip from the Gumballers? No because they are a secret!
What would be your ultimate Gumball car? Cayenne 4x4 Porsche.
Who would you bring as your co-pilot? My husband of course!
Sum up your impression of the Gumball in one word? Fous du Volant (Driving crazy)
And - what's it like to be famous? It's very nice, a bit like christmas all year round!

I'M FAMOUS!

25

Recognise me? I'm Adrien Brody

ROB DYRDEK WITH OBI-WAN BRODY

Oscar-winner Adrien Brody appeared on NBC's 'The Tonight Show with Jay Leno' on August 26th 2004. He spoke to Jay about cars, cops and how to cheat...

Please Welcome Adrien Brody, ladies and gentlemen...

Jay: I know you're a car guy because we always talk about cars, now tell me about this Gumball Rally you did in Europe.

Adrien: I drove 29 hours straight the first day with my friend, we were in a car for 32 hours, 29 hours of that was driving...

Jay: Wow!

Adrien: It's called the Gumball 3000 Rally because you drive 3000 miles within 5 days. We got lost so I did about 3500 miles in 4 and a half days.

Jay: In what kind of car?

Adrien: We had a Porsche Turbo.

Jay: Oh COOL!

Adrien: It was a rent-a-car.. I couldn't get anyone to give me a car so I had to rent one.

Jay: And what's the speed limit in Morocco.

Adrien: No speed limit in Morocco. Not when... well the King kind of granted us...

Jay: The King gives you a pass?

Adrien: Yeah the King kind of gave us a free pass!

Jay: See, this is why I like the monarchy. See that's good, the King gives you a pass and you can go as fast as you want.

Adrien: Pretty much.

Jay: Now how fast did you go? What's the fastest you think you went?

Adrien: (pause) ...I don't want to incriminate myself?

Jay: You can't.. what's the King gonna do.. come over here and slap the car?

Adrien: er..er... we kind of... yeah...we got it up to about 275/280 kilometres an hour, there were people going much faster though.

Jay: Did you get stopped by the cops?

Adrien: Oh yeah, I think everybody got stopped by the cops, we got pulled over seven times in four days.

Jay: Now see that would be excessive. Seven times in four days! Don't the cops call ahead and go 'hey there's this crazy guy coming...'

Adrien: Well yeah. Basically, once four, five, six cars all come by with racing stripes and numbers, they know there's more to come. They were very smart they just waited at the tollbooth so they didn't even have to catch you. You'd have to stop for a toll booth and then they'd go, [points and indicates to the side] very nicely, and you pull over.

Jay: So how many tickets did you get?

Adrien: Er, none. Not really, we

TWO SHADY CHARACTERS!

ADRIEN'S PORSCHE TURBO LEAVES THE GARAGE IN PARIS

made it out of a few situations. [Someone in the audience whoops] Yeah, thank you, it was an accomplishment!

Jay: How does one make it out of a few situations?

Adrien: In France it was interesting because I got pulled over and there were a number of other guys from the race who got pulled over and they were writing tickets. Then the one guy said 'Don't you know who he is? He's the Pianist" And the cop looked at me and goes 'aahhhh'. Then he points at me and goes, "Vous, you no pay. Vous, you pay!", to the guy who'd just hooked me up! Which is terrible [laughs]! I mean, he let me go which is crazy. It was really amazing. That's the best time to get recognised.

Jay: So who won the race?

Adrien: We finished first but we cheated [Jay laughs]. You know, everybody was getting pulled over so much, so by the time we got to Spain we were tired of it, so we left in the middle of the night. Everybody was supposed to leave in the morning, but we just decided to get there first. Get there early, the car was washed, we took a nap. Everybody showed up exhausted, and we were like, 'hi, wow, what took you so long?"

Jay: What a gruelling race!

Adrien: Yeah it was fun. I went with a buddy of mine from St Louis, Pat, and he assembled this....

[They show a clip from Rally]

Jay: Cool. I could do that!

Adrien: Yeah you should!

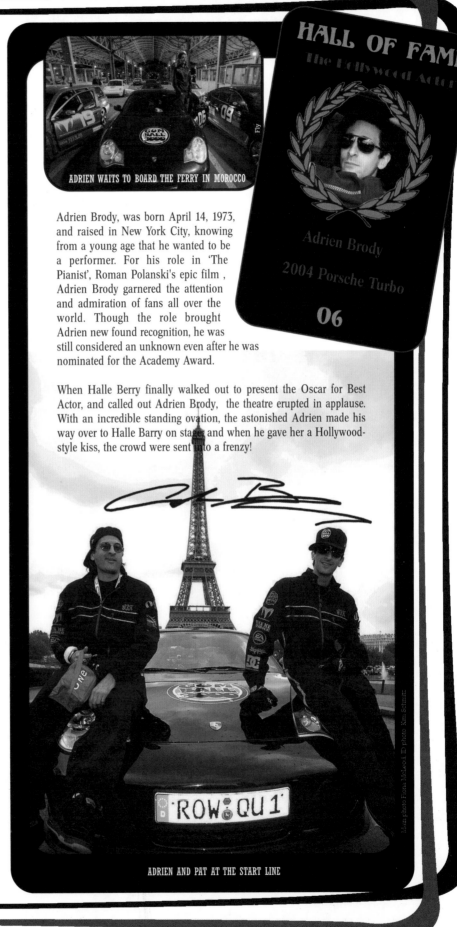

ADRIEN WAITS TO BOARD THE FERRY IN MOROCCO

HALL OF FAME
The Hollywood Actor

Adrien Brody
2004 Porsche Turbo

06

Adrien Brody, was born April 14, 1973, and raised in New York City, knowing from a young age that he wanted to be a performer. For his role in 'The Pianist', Roman Polanski's epic film , Adrien Brody garnered the attention and admiration of fans all over the world. Though the role brought Adrien new found recognition, he was still considered an unknown even after he was nominated for the Academy Award.

When Halle Berry finally walked out to present the Oscar for Best Actor, and called out Adrien Brody, the theatre erupted in applause. With an incredible standing ovation, the astonished Adrien made his way over to Halle Barry on stage and when he gave her a Hollywood-style kiss, the crowd were sent into a frenzy!

Main photo Fiona McLeod. ID photo Kim Schmitt

ADRIEN AND PAT AT THE START LINE

1. Cut out the car

2. Fold back the white tabs and glue down the sides of the car

3. Make sure the bottom is folded under and glued to the other side

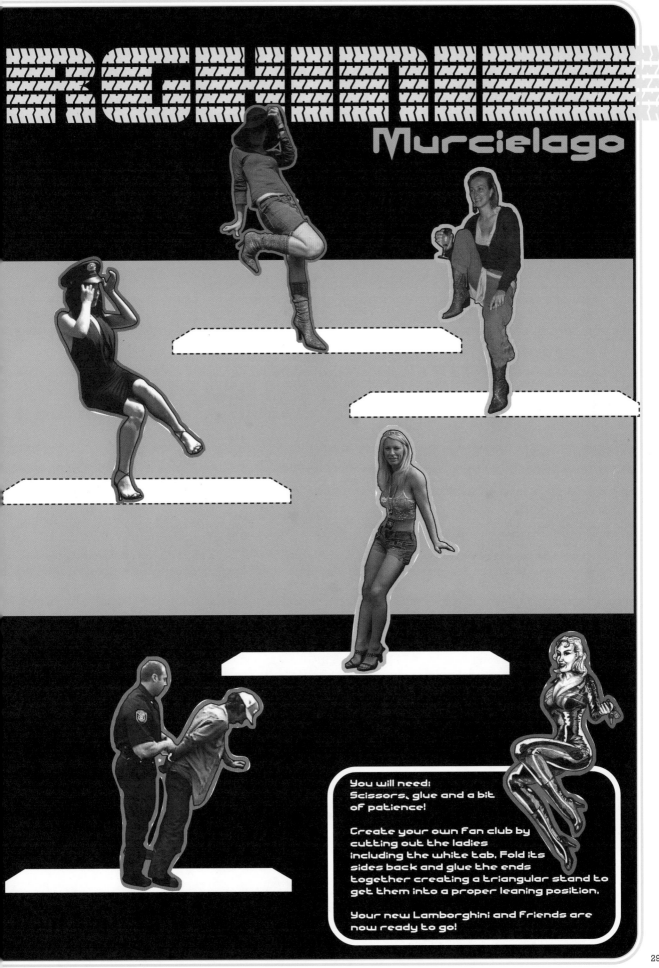

RGWNNE
Murcielago

You will need:
Scissors, glue and a bit
of patience!

Create your own fan club by
cutting out the ladies
including the white tab. Fold its
sides back and glue the ends
together creating a triangular stand to
get them into a proper leaning position.

Your new Lamborghini and friends are
now ready to go!

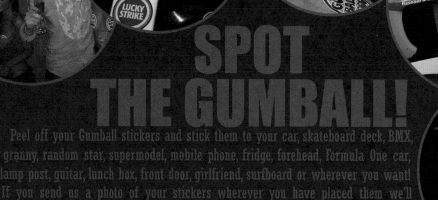

SPOT THE GUMBALL!

Peel off your Gumball stickers and stick them to your car, skateboard deck, BMX, granny, random star, supermodel, mobile phone, fridge, forehead, Formula One car, lamp post, guitar, lunch box, front door, girlfriend, surfboard or wherever you want! If you send us a photo of your stickers wherever you have placed them we'll put the photo on our website. The most random and uniquely placed stickers will win lots of Gumball goodies!

Either email your photo's to info@gumball3000.com or post them to the Gumball HQ (address at the front of the book).

GUMBALL BRAND JENSON BUTTONS BAR HONDA F1 CAR! DRIFTING CHAMPION CHRIS. FORSBERG ROCKS ONE! AND SO DOES F3000 CHAMPION ERNESTO VISTA! SHANE THE LE

MAX HAS THE RIGHT IDEA!

EVEN THE MONACO ROYALS HAVE GOT THE IDEA!

JOHNNY SPOTS A DECAL ON THE FAMOUS SPROOSE GOOSE PLANE!

NOW GET STICK

BUCKY, WINS YET ANOTHER GOLD!

YOU CAN WEAR IT AS A CAPE

ROAD SIGNS ARE GREAT TARGETS!

AS ARE OLD CARS!

AS ARE LAMP POSTS!

AND JOHNNY KNOXVILLE'S ARM!

ILLINOIS
ROUTE
66

30

GET LOST IN PARIS!!

SEE IF YOU CAN BEAT THE GUMBALLERS AS THEY TRY TO WEAVE THEIR WAY OUT OF PARIS!! (REMEMBER TO USE A PENCIL SO YOU CAN TRY AGAIN!)

C H E C K P O I N T :

Mas du Clos Race Circuit

CENTRAL FRANCE
5-6 MAY 2004
Checkpoint open:
10 pm - 1 am

Your first destination is at the magnificent private home and race circuit of Pierre Bardinon, one of the most beautiful circuits in the world.

The track was created in 1963, and over the years just about every racing team and champion driver has driven the circuit, so tonight's checkpoint and supper at Pierre's house is a real privilege.

Mileage: 250

Hours on road: 3-4

Total mileage: 250

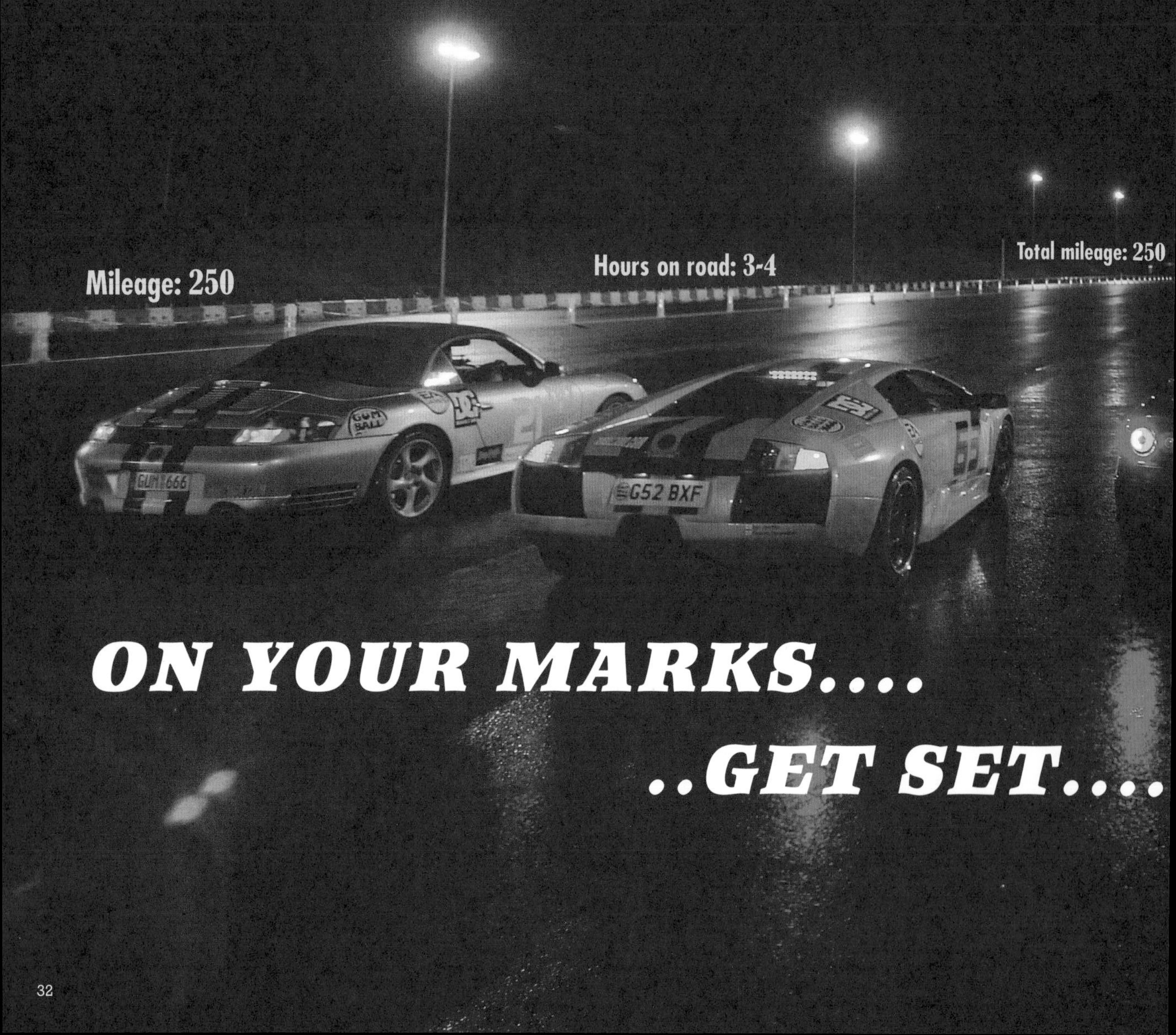

ON YOUR MARKS....

..GET SET....

Styletip: Wear your new Alpine Stars driving gloves to grip that steering wheel tightly.

"Pierre has the most amazing collection of Ferraris in the world!! We did a quick lap of the circuit before driving on through the night!

THIS IS NOT A TOY CAR!

...GO!

"Looking for adventure, get your motor running, get out on the highway..."

All photos: Fly

33

HALL OF FAME
Professional Skater

Willy Santos

1995 X-Games 3 rd place, 1997 Munster, Germany World Champion 1st place 1998 Vans Triple Crown 2 nd place, 2000 Willys Workshop Skateboard Barbershop opened

03

WARNING....

Willy Santos Speaks...

What's your daily ride? 1999 S80 Volvo or 1999 VW Eurovan.

What would be your ultimate Gumball car? 1993 Mitsubshi Expo.

A friend of mine said he skated a flatbar with Bucky in Marrakech. While you were in Morocco, did you find any good flat-bars in the Kazbar? That's a negative.

Did you find any undiscovered skate spot gems (Can you say that)? Yeah, can I please have the route cards again?

Are Gumballers scary? No, I'm scary!

Did you meet any bunnies? No, but I saw some pussy cats!

Who from history would be your dream Gumball co-driver? Indiana Jones.

What was your worst moment on the Gumball? Missing the ferry and not being able to change my underwear for 3 days.

What was your best moment on the Gumball? Passing cars on the shoulders in Morocco going 100 mph - was insane!

What, to you, is the Spirit of the Gumball? Getting lost.

Sum up your Gumball 3000 experience in one word? Crazy!!

Willy Santos

WILLY DOES THE GOOFY FOOT RAILSLIDE

ENTER AT OWN RISK!!
It's the' BIRDHOUSE®

From the beginning of Gumball, the skateboard industry has always played an integral part of the Gumball lifestyle and attitude, especially as Maximillion has been a skater since his early teens. Once skating in competitions and doing demos all over the world, Max now just skates to the office and back each day, sometimes via the odd skate park for some late night soul-seeking sessions. With this background it was inevitable that many skaters would end up taking part in the rally, and with Tony Hawk and Bucky Lasek's Gumball relationship over the years, it is no surprise that this year Birdhouse sent a 'team' of unprepared amateur skaters to witness the mayhem of Gumball first hand!

ANTHONY SHELTER
Professional Skater

MATT BALL
Professional Skater

JOE GOEMANN
Professional Skater

THE SKATERS 'GUMBALL' TRUCK

Matt Ball Speaks...
Home town: Las Vegas, Nevada.

What's your daily ride? 2003 Suzuki savage LS650 motorcycle, 83 Cadillac Deville.
Car driven in Gumball? Nissan Frontier.
Were there any special features or modifications? Steering wheel on wrong side!
What would be your ultimate

Mustang (the one that was in the rally).
How was your navigation through Europe?
It was very chaotic we didn't know what we were involved in, we assumed that all the directions were to be provided. We were pretty unprepared, we didn't even have a map to begin with!
What do you like to buy at gas rest-stops? Sodas and pocketknives!
What was your worst moment on the Gumball? Stuck in a French village by ourselves, and trying to communicate with the Frenchman fixing our car using hand gestures.
And your best moment? The first part of the trip, when we weren't behind everyone yet. We never made it to Africa, that sucked because I really wanted to. Our team manager

for Birdhouse, Seamus, put super-unleaded gas in our 'diesel' pick up truck and made it completely un-drivable! I went to this gas station and stole a hose while Seamus distracted the guy working there. We thought we could siphon the gas out of the engine, because we have seen it in movies our whole lives, but we found out the hard way that it doesn't work like that. All we got was a few mouthfuls of gas and and some very funny looking French policeman with moustaches. They were exactly like the guy in the Pink Panther cartoons. We finally got towed to some little shop and the guy pumped it all out. It took some time, so we skipped Morocco and decided to go straight to Barcelona, which wasn't too bad considering it is one of the best cities in the world to skate. We had a few days to skate, it was fun. I loved it.
Sum up your Gumball 3000

BUCKY WINS GOLD... AGAIN!
..AND AGAIN..

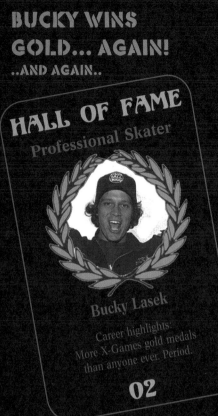

HALL OF FAME
Professional Skater

Bucky Lasek

Career highlights:
More X-Games gold medals
than anyone ever. Period.

02

What car did you drive on the Gumball? Well I started out in a Morgan Aero 8, the car was a right hand drive which meant you had to shift it with your left hand and I had no problem with that but the damn front end on the car was so long and you sat so low in the cockpit that seeing was nearly impossible with the rain. We made it to the first checkpoint after 'refuelling' and swapped the Morgan for a Range Rover. The reason for the swap was mainly because Willy my co-driver wasn't prepared for the

BUCKY WITH HIS SIGNATURE GUMBALL DECK

right hand drive and left hand shift of the Morgan. So, if I wanted any driving relief I had to sacrifice performance for the Range! *[It must also be noted that Bucky's co-driver, fellow skater Willy Santos was perhaps not the best navigator considering he slept 20 hours each day! (sorry Willy!!)]*

How much did you spend on fuel? The Range ate it up like air. Birdhouse gave me fuel money ($450 American) they thought would go awhile. It lasted just over a day!

What was your top speed? Morgan (40 km maybe in Parisian rain!) Range Rover (topped out at 160 km).

Did anything break on the car? Just my patience!

What's your dream Gumball car? Something sporty with a good suspension, brakes, a good top speed and room inside for 3.

What was the best moment on the Gumball? I enjoyed Morocco. Cruising around town all 6 of us on Karta's BMW (Bike). Honestly I don't even know how many we had on it but it was insane. We didn't even get pulled over. I think its because we were still doing the speed limit, so they thought it was cool.

What was your worst moment on the Gumball? Missing the ferry out of Morocco that also meant missing the F1 race. Booooo.

Did you fight with your co-driver? No, not with him but man I was sick of myself.

Who would be your dream co-driver? My wife naked!!

Tell me a little story about your Gumball experience? Well this year was more of an endurance test. One of my less than stressful moments had to be following the yellow Ferrari Enzo through the hillsides of Morocco. It was beautiful.

Marks out of 10 for this year's experience? 9, there was definitely room for improvement! See ya next year!

Bucky Lasek first picked up a skateboard at the age of 12. Soon after he was competing in amateur contests and quickly climbed up the ranks as a professional skateboarder. He is considered one of the world's most consistent vert skateboarders with a contest repertoire that includes more difficult tricks than any other skater competing today and he continues to place in the top three in competitions world wide collecting more medals than he knows what to do with!

Off the ramp, Bucky has a huge passion for cars and original Vespa's. He drives a very sweet AC Schnitzer BMW M3 (E46) SMG everyday, and after participating in the 2003 rally in a tuned Jaguar CEC Nothelle S-Type, has become the natural 'Action Sports' Ambassador to Gumball. This year Bucky alternated between a Range Rover Vogue and Morgan Aero 8, stating, "this years Rally was much more trying than the 2003 one in the States, especially when you only speak English and you can't read S$#!"!

BUCKY OLLIES JACOB IN MOROCCO

Al-Ya Boys

MAD DOG OLLIES BUCKY

Al-Ya Boys

DON'T TRY
THIS AT HOME

Tony Hawk was nine years old when his brother changed his life by giving him a blue fibreglass banana board. By twelve, Tony was sponsored by Dogtown skateboards, by fourteen he was pro, and by sixteen Tony Hawk was the best skateboarder in the world. In the ensuing 17 years, Hawk has entered an estimated 103 pro-contests. He won 73 of them, and placed second in 19. By far the best record in skateboarding's history.

In 1992 he started a skateboard company, Birdhouse Projects, with former Powell pro, Per Welinder, and in 1998 he and his family started a company called, of course, Hawk Clothing, which was acquired by Quiksilver in early 2000. In 1999 Activision and Tony created Tony Hawk's Pro Skater video game for PlayStation. They expected decent sales, but the copies blew off the shelves and has become one of the best-selling video-game franchises of all time. He still skates almost every day, still learns new tricks, and does public demos all year round. One of the reasons Tony decided to stop 'competing' at the end of 1999 was that he landed the first-ever 900 (two and a half mid-air spins) at the X Games. The 900 was the last on a wish list of tricks he'd written a decade earlier. Tony has taken part in the Gumball for the past two years, entering a 2003 Dodge Viper last year, and this year in Europe he and girlfriend, Lhotse, put the new Morgan Aero 8 through its paces!

HALL OF FAME
Skateboard Legend

Tony Hawk
Career highlights:
Winning a few competitions,
being on the Simpsons,
and having a signature video game

02

TONY WITH HIS MORGAN AERO 8
(ACTUALLY IT BELONGS TO CHARLES MORGAN)

How did this rally compare to previous ones you have done in the US? There was less concern for strict highway laws and overzealous cops, and the cars were much more exotic. **Did you find any amazing skate spots on the route?** The skatepark in Marbella was pretty good, and Barcelona has plenty of terrain.
Any tips on how to stay stylish on the Gumball? Accept the disheveled, sleepless, no shower look and go with it!
What do you by at gas rest stops? Gummi cola bottles!

What was your worst moment on the Gumball? After six straight hours of speedy-but-careful driving, pulling into the hotel in Spain and rear-ending the BMW in front of me! **What was your best moment?** The starting line. You can feel the adrenaline and horsepower itching to be unleashed.
What to you is the Spirit of the Gumball? Enjoying the journey as much as the destination.
Sum up your Gumball 3000 experience in one word? Fast!

Main photo: Atiba Jefferson

MADRID, SPAIN
6 May 2004

Checkpoint Open:
6am – 12noon

We strongly advise you keep to the route we suggest, crossing the Pyrenees at night via alternate routes is not scenic and is very dangerous.

In Madrid simply ask anyone for directions to the best known football club in history.

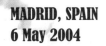

GUMBALLERS ENJOYED A COFFEE AND CROISSANT IN THE PRESIDENT'S SUITE OVERLOOKING ONE OF THE WORLD'S MOST FAMOUS BITS OF GRASS.

Hours on road: **6-10**

C·H·E·C·K·P·O·I·N·T:
Real Madrid Football Stadium

Total Miles: **890**

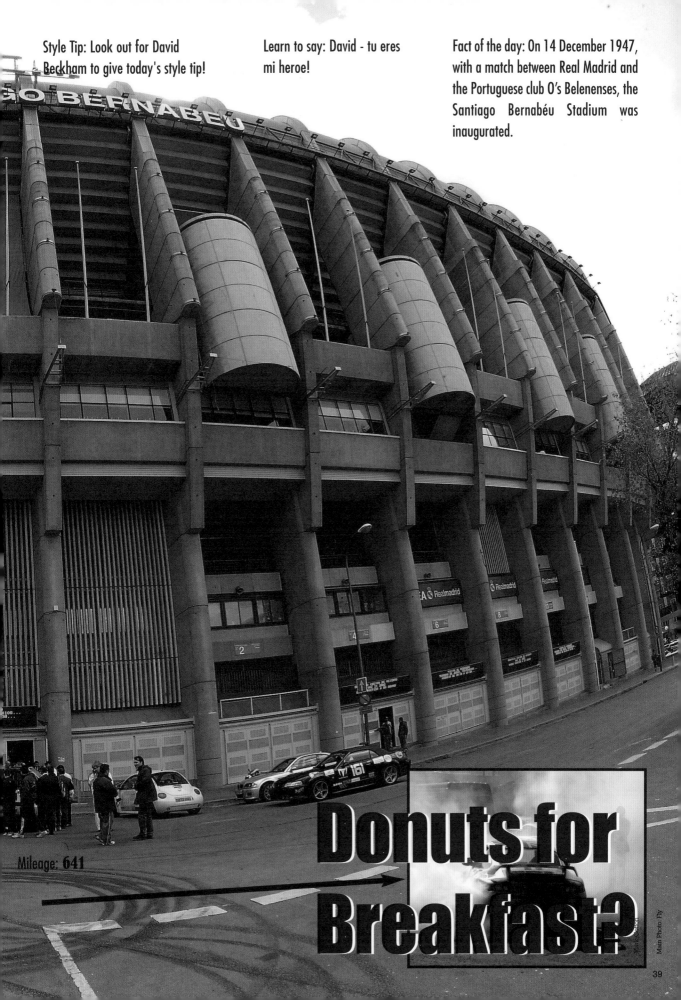

Style Tip: Look out for David Beckham to give today's style tip!

Learn to say: David - tu eres mi heroe!

Fact of the day: On 14 December 1947, with a match between Real Madrid and the Portuguese club O's Belenenses, the Santiago Bernabéu Stadium was inaugurated.

Mileage: **641**

Donuts for Breakfast?

Main Photo: Fly

SMOOTH OPERATOR

PERFORMANCE
Text & Co-driver: Sarah Donohue

Max speed:	198 mph
0-60:	4.7 sec
Max power:	552 bhp
Miles per gallon:	11/16 mpg
Engine capacity:	5998cc, W-12 Cylinder/ 6ltr twin turbo
Cost when new:	$197,000
Total produced:	n/a

As the co-driver, I took over from Michael when he was tired, which was perfect timing because when he got in the passenger seat he was asleep within about 45seconds!!! I found the car great to handle. My previous experience has been purely track days (all at major tracks). I very rarely drive on the road and I'm not actually used to driving slow, so the Gumball was perfect. My background is 11 years of racing powerboats, which has ZERO similarity to cars, and the Bentley was like driving in an armchair. Powerboats virtually tear the spine apart!

In most performance cars it's hard to hold a conversation at speed because of the noise, well this was quiet as a mouse and comfortable? I had the back massager on whilst driving…nearly fell asleep myself! And she handles perfectly. I'm a big one for braking systems and it's usually the first thing I notice on a car because I like to approach corners as fast as possible, leaving the braking as late as possible before I turn in. So stamping on the brakes and getting the perfect reaction is what I notice, and she sits lovely in braking. Oh yes! Perfect car choice! 3000miles in a feather pillow…

Car 09:
Driver: Michael Ross
Co-drivers:Sarah Donohue Emma Payne
SARAH ON HER FEATHER PILLOW

A Cheetah in Gen

Car 52:
Driver: Oliver Morley
Co-driver: Marina Kalukaite

Often overshadowed in the past by its luxury car partner Rolls Royce, Bentley has since stolen the limelight and the company was bought out by the VW Group in 2002. Although the Bentley Continental GT uses some of the German manufacturer's parts, such as the VW W12 engine, as a base, it is still a fine example of British class, elegance and engineering refinement. The 6-litre engine has been refitted with twin turbos, while the six-speed gearbox can be manually shifted with paddles mounted on the steering wheel. It is meant as an everyday car for an everyday gentleman, but there is something not so genteel about a vehicle that can get from 0-60mph in 4.7 seconds (quite a feat considering it's as heavy as some SUVs) and has a maximum speed of 198mph. In fact, the GT is more like a high performance sports supercar parading in gentlemen's clothing. The car achieves this dapper appearance, reminiscent of the 1952 Bentley R-Type Continental, with the help of numerous handcrafted touches that amount to 200 man

WO himself said that "The company's activities, particularly in its racing, attracted the public's fancy

Michael Ross

lemans Clothing!

Nick Price

2004 BENTLEY Continental GT

hours of labour to produce each car. When you think that most cars these days are built in a flash by robotic production lines, that's an awful lot of attention to detail. Among these touches are the 17 matched hides of leather used on the main interior surfaces (including a handstitched steering wheel), the real wood veneers and the chromed controls and grille. For comfort, a self-levelling air system takes care of the suspension while the seats feature heating and massage functions. When the GT reaches a certain speed a spoiler is automatically raised at the back to help keep the rear end down, however, Bentley does not advertise the actual speed that triggers the spoiler – probably for legal reasons!

and added a touch of colour, vicarious glamour and excitement to drab lives."

Car 140:
Messers: Kevin Jones, Ian Quest, Adrian Butler and Richard Harrison

GOD BLESS THE QUEEN

Fly

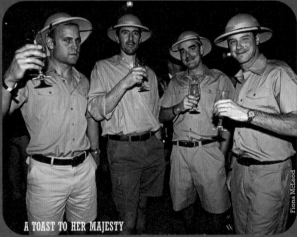

A TOAST TO HER MAJESTY

Fiona McLeod

THE BENTLEY BOYS

It is true that without the cars there would have been no "Bentley Boys"; but it is equally true that the "Bentley Boys" lent excitement, drama and prestige to their cars. Hard driving on the track, they played hard in their leisure time. They were amateurs of the old school, gifted sportsmen who competed not for monetary reward, but out of bravado and the thrill of the chase!

"GOLLY, WE'VE ARRIVED!"

Steve Hutton

COOL BRITANNIA

Gumball Factor: ★★★★☆

2004 CATERHAM R400 SV Superlight

Car 77:

Text and driver: Oliver Wheeler
Co-driver: David Smith

My co-driver Dave Smith and I knew it was a brave move taking an open-top Caterham Superlight on the Gumball. This became obvious during a torrential night of rain, sleet and zero-visibility through rural France. It felt like speedboat racing at night. The rest of the adventure was pure driving heaven and nothing beats piloting a Superlight through the undulating and twisting roads of North Africa. The combination of power and handling is awesome and it is surprisingly comfortable. The steering is so immediate and responsive that dodging stray camels at 130mph became second nature. We were only slightly put off by men with machineguns stopping us for t-shirts and stickers. The cops pulled us over eight times in total but loved the car so much we were only fined once. At the end of the trip, when we were shown to a reserved spot right in front of the entrance to the Carlton Hotel to rapturous applause and flashbulbs, Dave and I decided that there wasn't a single car on the rally we would rather drive. We have already ordered a newer and faster Superlight EVO for next year.

DAVID VS. GOLIATH

Blue vs. Green PERFORMANCE

Max speed (mph):	135	140
0-60 (seconds):	3.5	4.0
Max power (bhp):	200	190
Miles per gallon (mpg):	20	25
Engine capacity (cc):	1796	1796
Cost when new:	$40k	$40k
Total produced:	100	n/a

"CHOCS AWAY!"

In 1957 Colin Chapman fulfilled his dream of producing a 'four-wheeled motorbike' when his company Lotus made the original Seven. Ten years later, Caterham Cars in Surrey became the sole distributor for the Seven and has since continued to develop it under the Caterham name, making it the longest-produced car still on sale in Europe. The lightweight construction and incredible acceleration helped the Seven to make its mark on the racetrack, so much so in fact, that the RAC banned it from racing in 1976 saying it was "too fast". Since then four racing championships devoted entirely to the Caterham Seven have been established. The eye-catching 'this-car-means-business' styling also made its mark on the British public's imagination, as it appeared in the cult 1960s TV show The Prisoner.

The Sevens driven in the Gumball are modern, superlight versions weighing in at only 490kg each, enabling even more ferocious acceleration and responsive handling. In comparison to some of the luxury saloons (and, for that matter, most of the other vehicles) taking part in the Gumball, the Seven might not offer the ultimate in comfort but for pure novelty value and, therefore, 'Gumball factor' this hand-built British sportscar scores high.

CATERHAM
Four Wheeled Motorcycle

Car 119:
Text and drivers: Richard and Garry Gatt

This little car didn't miss a beat during the whole rally, however big brother's decision to leave the roof at home proved a tad stupid considering it rained pretty much non-stop from Paris to Madrid! Over the Atlas Mountains the Caterham came into it's own as a hill climber and we had some real fun around the outside of a few Porsches and

2002 CATERHAM 7 Superlight R

Ferraris. However the soft compound Avon tyres on the rear didn't quite last the distance and got us collared by the gendarmes with only two hours to go to Cannes. So what! Turning up at the Carlton Intercontinental on the back of a flat bed lorry was original if not even a little bit cool!! Highs – hotel beds. Lows – Kevlar seats. Overall the Caterham lacked space and top-end speed, but for novelty value and keeping it real…it was unbeatable!!

Fiona McLeod

THANK GOD FOR THE WEATHER IN MARRAKECH

COOL BRITANNIA

Gumball Factor: ★ ★ ★ ★ ☆

Racing Legend

1974 JAGUAR E-TYPE V12

With its sweeping curves, enormous bonnet and powerful engine, the Jaguar E Type captured the spirit of the age when it was first released at the beginning of the swinging Sixties. Designed by Malcolm Sayer as an evolution of the racetrack D Type that had been driven to three consecutive wins in the Le Mans 24 hour race from 1955 to 1957, the E Type was introduced to the retail market as a 'road-going sports and grand touring car'. Sayer had brought his expertise in aircraft aerodynamics to the arena of car design using a wind tunnel to test the E Type's shape and resulting in a car that could achieve a speed of 150mph and was available to consumers at half the price of a comparable Aston Martin.

The Series 3 E Type, as featured in the Gumball, was introduced in 1971 with a new 5.3 litre Jaguar V12 engine – at the time the world's only mass-produced V12 engine. Lightweight versions were also produced for the racetrack, where the E Type followed its predecessor in clocking up numerous victories. The combination of speed and a design way ahead of its time made the E Type irresistible to the likes of legendary footballer George Best and Beatles guitarist George Harrison, who both owned one. In the 1960s, E Types appeared in the trippy TV series The Avengers and the films The Italian Job and Elvis' Viva Las Vegas. Since then the car has featured in The Blues Brothers (driven by British 1960s model Twiggy) and Austin Powers – International Man of Mystery, further confirming its status as an icon of 1960s Cool Britannia.

FINALLY THE BRITISH ARE POPULAR IN PARIS

XGF 220M

YOU KNOW YOU'VE OWNED A JAGUAR TOO LONG WHEN... Text: George Cohn

You always park downhill.

You get in a car and are surprised when all of the instruments work.

You tell your wife that you were out until 3AM because the car broke down.........and she believes you.

The family is no longer upset in having to share the dinner table with a bunch of SU parts.

You wash your hands BEFORE working in the engine compartment.

You'd rather give the family pit bull a bath than tune your SU carburetors again.

You allow four hours for a trip, 3 for repairs and 1 for driving.

You can unstick a jammed starter in the dark, in the rain, in 5 minutes and don't think it's a big deal.

There's no oil on the garage floor so you know the car's completely empty.

XGF 220M

"THE CAD!"

CAR 101: Text and drivers: David and James Martell

How did it perform?
Brilliantly. An exceptional British sports car. We kept being told in Paris that we would never make it to Cannes!

What was the best moment on the Gumball?
Driving from Marrakech to Nador via Fes. The mountains and towns and roads were spectacular. Some of the Ferrari 360s couldn't keep up with us on this leg. The E-type was in its element here, especially as it has far more ground clearance than all of the supercars so it wouldn't ground out on the sometimes poor road surfaces.

What was your worst moment on the Gumball?
Being concerned for the Gumballers involved in accidents.

Did you fight with your co-driver?
My co-driver was my son and we got on really well. He lives in America and the 10 days around the Gumball was the longest I had spent with him for 10 years.

Tell me a little story about your Gumball experience?
In Almeria, we calculated that we had 500 miles to cover in 5 hours if we were going to make the Barcelona grand prix. Whilst going round a sweeping left hand corner into a tunnel at 120mph, the right rear tyre blew out putting us completely sideways. Luckily I managed to hang onto the car and come to a controlled stop on the other end of the tunnel to change the tyre. It was a scary moment. The E-Type has no safety cells, air bags or roll cages...

PERFORMANCE

Max speed:	135 mph
0-60:	7.4 sec
Max power:	272bhp
Miles per gallon:	14 mpg
Engine capacity:	5343cc
Cost when new:	N/A
Total produced:	N/A

COOL BRITANNIA

Gumball Factor: ★★★☆☆

TX1 LONDON BLACK CAB

PERFORMANCE

Max speed:	105 mph downhill
0-60:	24.7 sec
Max power:	80 bhp
Miles per gallon:	25 mpg
Engine capacity:	2750 cc
Cost when new:	£32,500
Total produced:	10,000

It's a piece of doodoo. 2 tonnes, no brakes, no speed, no handling. People thought it was a Rolls Royce.

The Black Cab driven in the Gumball is the current London taxi, a model called the TX1 that first went on sale in 1997. London taxis are also known as 'Hackney Carriages' after the original taxis drawn by 'haquenee' horses that began operating in the city in the early 17th century.

The TX1 has to meet stringent regulations set up by the Public Carriage Office called 'Conditions of Fitness', which result in the vehicle gaining some unusual characteristics. Among these is an incredibly tight turning circle of 7.6m enabling cabbies to execute U-turns quickly in busy traffic and rear doors hinged at the back that are thought to discourage customers from running off without paying. The taxi also has easily replaceable bodywork panels to help it survive a life on the chaotic streets of the Big Smoke. Incidentally, there is no official requirement that London taxis are black, although most cabbies do opt for this famous colour over the other choices such as white and carmine red. Considering it was built for a high mileage, low speed, stop-start existence, the appearance of the TX1 in the Gumball is a testament to the questionable sanity of those driving it!

A CABBIE WRITES:

Text: Martin Greaves

HARRY ARTATAC

Gumball? You sure? In all my driving days, I've never seen nuffin like it. Nuffin. The waste, the ARROGANCE, the sheer bloody LIBERTIES they take!! They come over here – no one asked 'em – in their flash FOREIGN cars, and drive around my town with utter, utter, DISRESPECT!! I've seen 'em go thru RED lights like they don't give a toss, pardon my French. You could buy a house for what some of them bloody Lambos cost. It's OUTRAGEOUS!! A disgusting WASTE!! You could build a nice orphanage for that. But oh no, they don't think of the kiddies, do they? I had that Max in the back of my cab once. Lovely man!!

Car 138:
Driver: Martin Greaves
Passengers: Graham Taylor, Chris Crooks
Fare £9500 + tip!!!!

ZZZZZZZZZZZZZZZZZZZZZZ...YOU GET IT WHERE YOU CAN ON THE GUMBALL.....ZZZZZZZZZZZZZZZZ.ZZ

Two Saville Row tailors flag down a cab in London and give the destination, Marrakech

Where to Guv?

10 POINTS IF YOU HIT THE CAMEL UNDER PAR

THE FERRARI BROKE MY CONCENTRATION

Martin Greaves

The driver turned out to be Martin, an ex-cabbie, and a man mean enough to borrow his brother's cab to avoid paying the congestion charge. He was easily persuaded, and with his legitimate old licence (or "bill").

But a cab, obviously, is a bit of a duck out of water in the deserts of North Africa and the 150mph dashes across countries for lunch. The right to use the Euston Road bus lane doesn't help catch a GT2 in open country. However, it is exceptionally reliable, it's comfortable enough to catch up with sleep in the back, and it's able to become a tailor's fitting room at the popping of a champagne cork. Three things a Lambo isn't.

Paper was the only thing that almost stopped it. Because it was being driven just on the strength of Martin's bill (the way things are done in London) there were no hire papers, agreements, permissions, receipts or any of the bumf beloved by border police. In this case, police armed with rubber stamps and machine guns to valiantly defend Morocco from the illegal taxi importation trade. The cab simply was not going to get off the boat without paperwork that just didn't exist in Bethnal Green let alone the middle of the Gibraltar Straits. But Chris was not going to be beaten now. He found some paper. Deep down in the hold he found someone called Robert Maxwell who said he'd sign anything. And, amazingly, he found a typewriter in his own luggage. With paper, a typewriter and a Maxwell signature you could take over the world – or at least pass the border guard test. The cab got through.

When in Morocco it did have trouble keeping up on the first 200 miles of empty, no-speed-limit motorway, with the Enzo just managing to pull ahead after an hour or so! The mountains were more of a leveller, where driving rather than right-footing mattered. Here the cab hung in. The trusty Nissan engine boiled going up the hills, even with all the heaters blasting, and that awful smell on the way down turned out to be all that was left of the brakes. Thank the wonderful Moroccan police for holding up traffic because the cab couldn't stop. It made the ferry.

The highlight was careering round Circuit Paul Ricard. With only 80 horsepower dragging a couple of tons through a 3 speed auto, the plan was "momentum". Like a video game (except with the possibility of pain) the idea was to go flat out, hang on through the corners and hope the barge didn't flip over. On the first lap about three people on the viewing balcony watched the cab squeal round. The tyres and suspension complaining bitterly that this wasn't part of their deal. On the second lap there were dozens cheering as the cab four-wheel-drifted through some corners and the passengers were leaning yacht-style to try and stay on the track. The F1 Mercedes team, overnighting on the way back from Barcelona, applauded the cab off the circuit. Chris was a very happy tailor.

Text: Martin Greaves

FUNNILY ENOUGH THEY HAD NAVER SEEN A BLACK CAB ON THE TRACK

Cool Britannia

Text & Driver: Mark Schilling, Co-driver: Jeremy Baker

Max speed:	170 mph
0-60:	3.7 sec
Max power:	352 bhp
Miles per gallon:	13 mpg
Engine capacity:	2968 cc
Cost when new:	$95k
Total produced:	200 pr yr

The Noble was a drivers dream. Extremely quick, great handling, comfortable and most importantly, British! Mark and I shared the driving but the best seat was undoubtedly the driving one. The Noble received a lot of attention because of its fierce line and rarity.

In France I picked up my first speeding ticket ever – 169 kph. A 90 Euro fine and we were on our way. In the UK that would have been a ban... The best driving section was the second day in Morocco. The winding bends through the hills suited the cars abilities perfectly.

The best part was completing the whole rally with no mechanical issue at all.

A ROSE AMONG CARNATIONS

FERRY LOAD UP

2004 Noble M12 GTO R

It might not be the most famous brand of car in the Gumball but the Noble M12 still has the capacity to turn heads. It doesn't have the pedigree of a Porsche or a Ferrari but its performance is on a par with them and it is considerably cheaper to buy. Noble Cars are built in Leicestershire under the watchful eye of company boss and chief designer Lee Noble who was once a racing driver and was also involved in the development of McLaren's famous F1 supercar. He has since carved a distinct identity with his own cars, of which the M12 has proved his biggest success.

The GTO-3R version of the M12 can produce up to a whopping

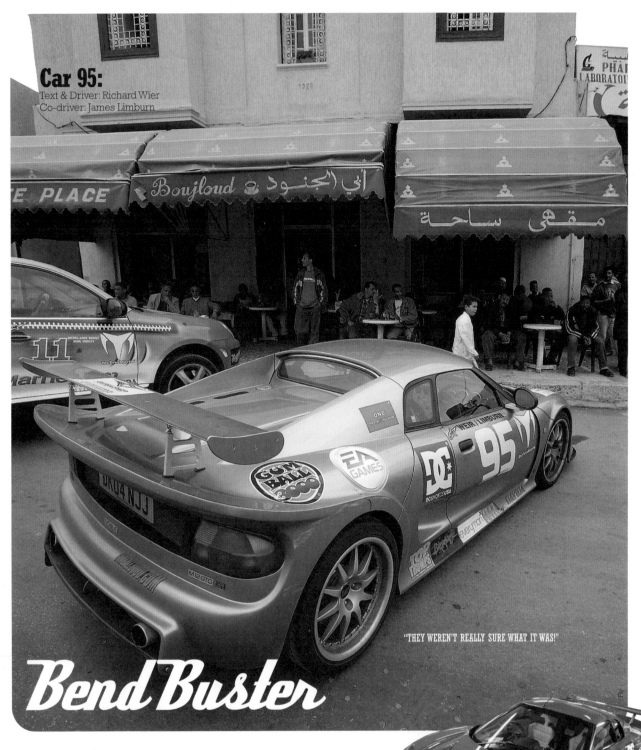

Car 95:

Text & Driver: Richard Wier
Co-driver: James Limburn

"THEY WEREN'T REALLY SURE WHAT IT WAS!"

Bend Buster

Nick Price

352bhp. However, one of the M12's in the Gumball had a full K04 upgrade, meaning it could produce over 450bhp and accelerate from 0-60mph in less than four seconds! In fact, even the standard M12 GTO-3R is one of very few cars available to the public that can get from 0-100mph in less than ten seconds. In addition to being cheaper than comparative cars in its class it's also easier to drive with supple suspension and confidence-inspiring handling. It's a good job because with all that power under the bonnet you'll need every bit of spare confidence you can find to really let this beast go!

COOL BRITANNIA

Gumball Factor: ★ ★ ★ ☆ ☆

The Endurance Drive Game

PARIS to MARBELLA

Total mileage since Paris: 1262
Hours on road: 20-36+

Initiate yourself into the 'Spirit of the Gumball' by playing the Endurance Drive Game. The goal is to get yourself from Paris to the South of Spain in time to join the big party at the Hotel in Marbella!

Directions: Carefully cut out the Burt Reynolds tokens below and choose a colour. Then take turns rolling a dice, follow the instructions when you land on a square.

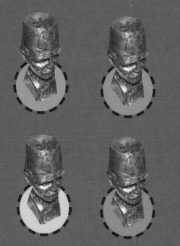

Gumbopoly

Just Visiting / Jail

Many drivers went off-piste on tiny w roads rather than taking the main motor route through the Pyrenees Mountains. Ad Brody reached Marbella at 2am, complai "I want to go home. This isn't what I thoug was gonna be like". Miss next turn.

Too tired to drive. Miss next turn.

The Ford Escort RS Rally car broke its gearbox after attempting a crowd-pleasing donut in Paris. Mechanics drove all night from England, with a new gearbox. The car finally hit the road and caught up. Such Gumball spirit deserves a bonus. Swap your Burt with whoever is in the lead

On trying to leave the car park in Paris, the battery of the NYPD police car was flat after using its' siren too much! Miss next turn.

Fiona McLeod

Old silver foxes, Hans Lautrup and co-pilot Kim Brangstrup, were the first to arrive in Marbella in a diesel powered BMW X3. They showered and played a round of golf before retiring to the bar to wait for everyone else!!
You win.

AFRICA!

GO

Blow a tire. Back 3 spaces.

Stop for gas. Miss next turn.

Caught speeding

Go to Jail

We followed the music out to the club in the heart of the hotel. We danced the night away and swapped stories with fellow Gumballers.

A Ferrari Enzo scratches a rim in Madrid. The owner has a new Enzo shipped over from Italy. For sheer ridiculousness roll again.

Got caught doing twice the speed limit. Spend the next three years in jail. Game over

Learn to say:
"Taxi, llevame al Hotel antes que pierdo mi sentido de humor (Taxi can I follow you to the hotel, I've lost my sense of humour)". Advance to Finish.

Here comes that spare part you ordered

Past the Rock of Gibraltar

..as seen in James Bond!

Finish

Join Party

If you arrive after 4am go straight to ferry

Main photo: Fiona McLeod. Surrounding photos thanks to everyone!

Hans Lautrup's

(5) Tips on handling an *Endurance Drive:*

1. Get a car with a big tank for fewer fuel stops!
2. Don't get lost - take your time, follow directions and read the map!
3. Take it nice n' easy... those who speed either get stopped by the police, or they're in such a hurry they miss their directions and go the wrong way!
4. Choose a good co-pilot that you get on with so you can take turns driving!
5. Don't bring any girls because your wife might find out when the film comes out!

Follow these guidelines and you'll be golfing in Marbella, waiting for the others to get there. Cheers!

CHECKPOINT:

Marbella

Hotel Puente Romano, Marbella, Spain
6 May 2004

This huge endurance drive has fully initiated you into the 'Spirit of the Gumball!'

No driving again till tomorrow so sleep tight!

Be in your car by 8.30am ready to depart for the Port of Algeciras.

NEXT STOP AFRICA!

To Gumball
God Bless you!
with yo' Badd!!!
Self!
Love Kym Mazelle
2004

Kym Mazelle grew u
around the corner fro
one of pop music's reignir
dynasties, the Jackson's, ar
early interactions wi
Michael, Janet, Tito, LaToya ar
the rest undoubtedly marke
Kym as a future diva.

Initially, she set out to become a div
in the true sense of the word b
studying opera at the Mundelein Colleg
of music in Chicago, Illinois, befo
moving into the pop world. After gainir
global recognition with a number
successful singles under her belt, sh
released her debut album, Crazy, in 198
establishing herself as one of hous
music's favourite divas. A collaboratic
with soul II soul produced the sing
Missing You, drawing even more attentic
to her talents, and in 1991she switched
EMI'S Parlophone and released her U.
debut album, Brilliant!

Kym's international status was recognize
again as she was featured on the high
successful soundtrack to the 1996
Blockbuster movie 'Romeo & Juliet' w
Young Hearts Run Free.

Showing no signs of slowing down, Ky
has become a constant within the eve
changing landscape of dance mus
as well as a regular participa
since 2000 on the Gumba

HALL OF FAME
Soul Diva

Kym Mazelle

Career highlights:
Soul II Soul- Back to Life
Romeo & Juliet's- Young Hearts Run Fr

03 & 153

Lay Jeno Speaks

The Diva
KYM MAZELLE

LJ: So did you sing at all the parties?
Kym: I was supposed to but I missed half th
stops! I perfomed in Paris and I sang
Cannes with Norman. Norman Dj'd and I ju
freestyled. Oh, and I sang the blues in th
middle of nowhere in Morocco.

LJ: Car driven in Gumball?
Kym: Started in the back of a
NYPD police car, ended up i
chauffeur driven limo i
Morocco. Then with Buck
and Willy (Birdhous
Skaters) at the end.
I don't know how to drive
car I never have to drive.
but then I constantly hav
to talk to keep the drive
awake. They're drainin
your energy and you're lik

Story time with....
KYM MAZELLE
The Mother Diva

When I woke up in Marbella nearly everyone had left, so now I'm standing there, no car and no driver… and I see this big guy, like 6ft5, standing at the side of the road, with all his bags around him and he's crying like a baby, "I wanna carry on the Gumball, I wanna finish the Gumball." Apparently

Baby - I called him baby - he and his friends had lost the Limo they were in. But I wasn't about to wait around, I got the hotel to call me a cab to go catch the boat. But I'm a mother right, so I hug him, and I say, "baby, don't cry, come with me in the car. This is Gumball, it'll be fine. We'll find people with cars to put your friends in, we'll get you all to the port to get the boat to Morocco."

But there must have been MORE people that didn't have rides because they all heard me and started running to the car going 'We're going with Kym, we're going with Kym", and I'm like "I don't have that many cabs!" But anyway, we picked up another guy on the way too with his Lotus wrapped around something… he'd had an accident.. So there's me at the port with the 10/11 stranded people that I had picked up along the way… And of course we missed the first boat and had to wait for the second one. But I managed to get the limo back and I piled everybody in the limo!

The Limo was great, it was an old-fashioned American limo that could seat 12 people, At first we are 2 and then it ended up being 6, 7 of us in the back and we had DVD player, the music, the disco lights, vodka cigarettes… I watched the Gumball movie in the back of the limo going across morocco, drinking champagne. It was so surreal.

So I didn't get to see any souks in Morocco. But I did go to the club! When we finally got to Marrakech I was so desperate, I went "I'm going upstairs and changing and finding a club, I don't care, I'll make one in the lobby. I'm going out!". Another Gumballer, Momo had a club in Marrakech, so I went there.

The next morning I got in the car with Bucky and Willy the Birdhouse Skaters. Willy found out I was in Soul II Soul and he didn't shut up, after that he was just like Oh my God 'baack to life', and then I found out they were skateboarders and that Willy's got Willywear and Bucky's got Buckywear and I exchanged CDs with them in return for clothes for my nephew! We had so much fun, but then we missed the boat again in Morocco to get back to Spain. We drove and drove and drove and we were this close… we watched the boat sail away and… Bucky lost it. He got lost in the

fatigue, you know, the Gumball thing that happens, the strain,(that's the part that I like!).

So here we are again, missed the boat, we're sitting on the side in the middle of no-where in Morocco and what else can a diva do but start singing the blues! Then, this guy turns up out of nowhere going, 'I know Max I know Max, come with me, Max is my friend', someone had given him one Gumball sticker, and he was working his deal with this sticker, 'I am Gumball, I know Max, I know Max, official Gumball, I take you for food, I take you for drink. You want something to drink, you want something to smoke, I take you, I know Max, I am Gumball'. He found us clean bathrooms, and food and a hotel and we were saved.

'okay I'm gonna take a nap now' and they're like 'no, no, no talk to me!'

J: Define diva on the Gumball?
Kym: Diva is everything. Mother, sister, party person, someone who's there if you need something, if the rooms run out at the hotel, if you need a room to party, keeping people awake, always happy, singing. I was more like another Diva on this Gumball because there were so many people to look after.

J: What does a diva wear on the Gumball?
Kym: I brought twenty pairs of shoes on the Gumball this year. It was so stupid.

J: How many did you wear?
Kym: One! Julien MacDonald made me a special dress but I didn't get to wear it. He made me this complicated thing that I just couldn't wear (sorry Julien). I just wanted to wear my jeans. I planned all these outfits but missed every event that I was gonna wear them at! I just ended up wearing the Gumball racesuit, that I loved.

lost my playboy jacket on the Gumball and my trench coat. You loose so much stuff on the

Gumball because you're just getting up and running from place to place and leaving really quickly and you leave all your stuff behind.

Next year, I want all the outfits. I'll need a car for all my costume changes, bring lots of wigs. I need to be more extreme diva next year, I've been talking to theatre people about outfits.

LJ: Any Diva style tips?
Kym: Cat suits, jump suits, adidas tracksuits, voyage tracksuits are really comfortable it doesn't wrinkle, so you still look stylish when you have to get up at four in the morning and get petrol and the cameras are still rolling and the Gumball hats.

Ladies, good to have your Prada shoes for the evening events but for the day I would say trainers or good cowboy boots. Wear a short skirt and show your legs off, if they look good!!

LJ: What is the Spirit of The Gumball to you?
Kym: Anything goes. We Gumballers look out after each other. The Gumball raises your edge. We're gonna see what happens and we're gonna have a good time. You might not even get to the end of it. It's an endurance test.

I got about 15 people who wanna do the Gumball with me next year because they're like, 'Kym all you talk about is the Gumball!'

I'm a Gumballer! Once you've been gumballed, it gets inside you!'

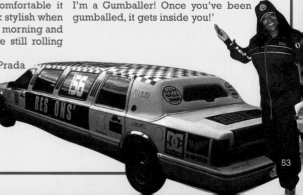

In the port in Tangiers, two blacked out Peugeot 406's from the Moroccan secret service are waiting for the Gumballers to dock. As the cars drive off the ferry, the King's Chief of Security greets them. His message:

"We are here to look after you until you leave the country, and will be by your side for the whole trip .... Oh, and the King says hi."

With the King of Morocco a fan of the Rally and personal friend of a pair of Gumballers, friendly policemen were placed at each junction along the route to wave Gumballers along and keep them from getting lost.

Welcome to MOROCCO

CHECKPOINT:
Casablanca

RICK'S CAFE
CASABLANCA, MOROCCO
7 MAY 2004

Checkpoint open: Midday-17:00
Prepare to enter another continent and a different world.

Lunch will be at the famous 'Rick's Café' which Humphrey
Bogart put on the map in the 1940s classic movie
'Casablanca'. With Sam playing on the piano, relax
and watch the ceiling fans turn as you enjoy
your first taste of Moroccan tea.

Sightseeing: By far the most impressive
sight in Casablanca is the Hassan II Mosque
- reputed to be the biggest in the world.
It's the only mosque in Morocco that
non-Muslims can visit - we highly
recommend it!

RICK'S CAFE

2004 PORSCHE CAYENNE

STANDARD CAYENNE

With a top speed of 165mph, this luxury vehicle is definitely at the sporty end of the Heavyweights category. With the Cayenne, the German sportscar-meisters, have translated their technological expertise into the off-road arena extremely well. Its classy looks tell nothing of its rugged off-road performance capability as it can climb or descend any slope with up to a 45 degree angle. The Cayenne also offers the ultimate in comfort no matter what terrain it's tackling thanks to its Porsche Active Suspension Management system that continuously adjusts the damping of the pneumatic suspension according to the external conditions and the individual driver's style.

GUMBALL CAYENNE GEMBALLA GT700

The Cayenne used in the Gumball was a special version modified by the German company Gemballa. It features an upgraded engine gearbox, improved braking system, additional bodykit for improved aerodynamics, lowered suspension and lighter alloy wheels.

PERFORMANCE

Max speed:	186 mph
0-60:	4.5 secs
Max power:	700 bhp
Miles per gallon:	12 mpg
Engine capacity:	4500cc
Cost when new:	$1m
Total produced:	9

ENGINE TROUBLE....

In Marrakech, the gearbox went on the White Porsche Cayenne Gemballa, the Rally's most expensive million dollar car, bought and customised especially for the Rally. The owner had a jet fly from Riyadh to Porsche in Germany, pick up mechanics and a gearbox, fly to Marrakech where they worked overnight, right in front of the hotel.

Text: Tom Trinkle

Car 15:

Text and driver: Sultan Al-Sagaggaf
Co-driver: Raid Bagedo, Ali Amrane,
Talal Al-Romaih, Dass-Belkecem Guerar

How did your car perform?
700BHP and 1100lb/ft of torque..
We were beating everyone.

Did anything break on the car?
Yeah. The gearbox died twice.
The first time was on the way to
Marrakech, I had another one
flown out from Germany in my jet
and they changed it in the hotel
car park overnight. It broke again
on the way to the ferry in Nador
but we continued with only 3
gears instead of 6 and still
finished 27th!

**Would you do the Gumball in it
again?**
No.

**What car are you entering next
year?**
A 700bhp Brabus Smart car and a
helicopter.

**How much did you spend on
fines?**
Nothing.

**What was your best moment on
the Gumball?**
The drive from Madrid to
Marbella. We were kicking it,
open roads and flying past
everyone. Even the
Murcielago was having

trouble when we dropped a gear!

**What was your worst moment on
the Gumball?**
We were trying to clock 310km/h
(194mph) and at 260km/h
(163mph) the gearbox went

**Did you fight with your co-
drivers?**
No. We were a cool group.

**Who would be your ultimate co-
driver?**
Michael Schumacher.

**Tell us something about your
Gumball experience?**
Everyone was so nice on the
Gumball. When we broke down,
everyone stopped to see if they
could help in any way.

**Marks out of 10 for your Gumball
experience?**
9.

**Marks of 10 for your cars
performance?**
8.

THE PRINCESS AND THE PORSCHE

After chasing after her
brother's private jet in her
own plane (apparently
they're a two jet
family), this Saudi
Princess arrived in
Paris in time to take part
in the rally. Her brother,
however, didn't want her
to enter, so against his
wishes she bought a
standard Cayenne and
participated with her
bodyguard anyway!

SULTAN OF THE GARAGE

ROYALE....

"BLING BLING"

"$*#&%$#&*$*% SAME OLD UNRELIABLE GERMAN MACHINERY!!"

Main photo: Renton

HEAVY WEIGHTS

Gumball Factor: ★★★★☆

57

Driving the Hummer Big Brother style.

Spillie, winner of one of the original Big Brother reality TV series in Belgium, was slowly cruising behind a Gumballer driving a silver Ferrari Maranello that was, in turn, stuck behind a Moroccan cement truck. There were many oncoming cars so Spillie decided to overtake them both on the right-hand side. The 5 metre-width of gravel next to the asphalt meant there was enough space even for the Hummer to pass. However, some 30 metres further ahead, Spillie spotted a huge water puddle in the gravel area and decided to wait so that he overtook the Ferrari while driving through the puddle. The puddle turned out to be a lot deeper than he thought. Never mind! A massive wall of water and mud spat out in front and around the Italian sportscar! Spillie then broke into a frenzied fit of laughter and looked over at his co-driver, to laugh about the huge wave of mud that engulfed the Ferrari. His co-driver, however, shot him a stern look and asked if Spillie had seen the pavement full of Moroccan people dressed in white, drinking cups of tea that he had also splashed.

Three quarters of an hour later, the Hummer was forced to stop for a re-fuel, as was the almost unrecognisable Maranello. "Did I do that?" Spillie asked in a kiddie voice. The Maranello driver replied, "Why me? Why me?" and added in true Gumball Spirit, "Cool idea BUT my f***ing window was open!!"

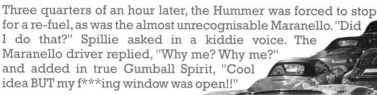

HUMMER H2

PERFORMANCE

Text and driver: Spillie Venderbean
Co-driver: Peter Jules, Frederik Dusesoi, Sabine dubois

My Navi System was extremely accurate in Paris because we came out first. My Car was very slow BUT comfortable on the highway to Spain. (It also went almost off the road on the French circuit by taking the first corner when we arrived there at midnight). My Co driver and me were having the time of our life experience while crossing Morocco cause we overtook about every "Gummyballer" (Gummyballer = Gumballer Without Balls) with our Yellow Mud Eating Bulldozer and Yeah, last but not least, it was a babe and celebrity magnet at the Cannes Filmfestival.

Max speed:	100 mph
0-60:	7,5 secs
Max power:	340 bhp
Miles per gallon:	3 km per Liter
Engine capacity:	6.000 cc
Cost when new:	$93,000
Total produced:	N/A
Any modifications:	Borla Exhoust System, Kenwood Touch Screen DVD Navigation

DOES NOT PLA

The heroic Hummer looks for adventure.

At 6,900 pounds this is the heaviest of all the Heavyweights. It is an evolution of the original H1 High Mobility Multipurpose Wheeled Vehicle (HMMWV) or 'Hummer' for short that was built for use by the US military and has seen service in many warzones. The H2 used in the Gumball is a slightly more refined version for the civilian market but it still has the hardcore feel of the original military-issue vehicle.

The Hummer is so huge that driving it in urban areas can be a real hassle. At 86.5 inches wide, drive-thru burgers are not an option, neither are many toll roads, petrol stations and car parks. Despite its mammoth proportions, the Hummer can be driven comfortably at speeds of 70-80 mph thanks to its four wheel independent suspension and enormous 37 inch tires. On the interior, however, the Hummer is less forgiving with a very cramped seating arrangement. Another disadvantage is the vehicle's almost unquenchable thirst for petrol – it even has two fuel tanks! The Hummer may well be best suited to long, slow slogs over the rough terrain of a battlefield but its eye-catching looks and its undeniable presence on the road also perfectly represent the true Gumball spirit...

WELL WITH OTHERS

"$10,000 OF FUEL LATER WE ARRIVED IN CANNES!"

86

Car 86:
Driver: Mark Kershaw
Co-driver: John Foley, Stephen Byrne, Robard Lyne

THE HUMMER SQUEEZES INTO THE ANCIENT MEDINA IN FEZ

HEAVY WEIGHTS

Gumball Factor: ★★★☆☆

8pm cocktails
followed by dinner.
Afterwards, in the heart of the
old town at the exotic Djemaa El Fna
Square, snake charmers
will vie with fortune tellers for your
attention. Then entry to Morocco's
hottest club will be with your
Gumball ID.

6am breakfast.
Ready in your car at 8am.

Marrakech

بوسكورة
BOUSKOURA

مراكـش 210
MARRAKECH

Tips: Be prepared for this crowded, chaotic, noisy yet enchanting Imperial City. Children and locals will harass you from the second your car arrives at the hotel, they will be enthusiastic to see so many amazing cars. As if the Gumball wasn't enough- the intensity of this town will leave you exhausted.

Sequence: Fiona McLeod

Hotel Kempinski Mansour Eddahbi
MARRAKECH

Mileage: **96**   Hours on road: **2-4**   Total mileage: **1559**

Fiona Mcleod

Christopher Livingstone Eubank is a former British boxing champion. On November 18 1990 he beat Nigel Benn to become WBO Middleweight Champion, and September 21 1991 beat Michael Watson to become WBO Super Middleweight Champion, which he remained until 1995.

Eubank and his wife, Karron, have four children, and in 2003 they invited television cameras to follow their lives for nine-months; the resulting show, 'At Home With The Eubanks', was broadcast on Five as the UK's answer to 'The Osbourne's'. Chris' public image is one of an eccentric, and he is known for his lisp and foppish fashion-sense, often wearing a monocle and carrying a cane.

Chris and Karron took part in the very first Gumball back in 1999, driving his enormous Peterbilt Truck. The truck's top speed was limited by the 'govnor' and as such Chris and Karron didn't arrive to any of the venues until hours after the rest of the cars had eaten, partied and gone to bed! Nevertheless, when they did arrive everyone knew about it as Chris used the airhorn of the truck to maximum effect, waking everyone up!
His style and commitment to the adventure instantly made him a Gumball favourite, winning the prestigious 'Spirit of the Gumball' in that inaugural year.
They have since participated in 2000 and came back for more this year. With his mix of sporting prowess and eccentric manner, Chris will always embody the Gumball spirit!

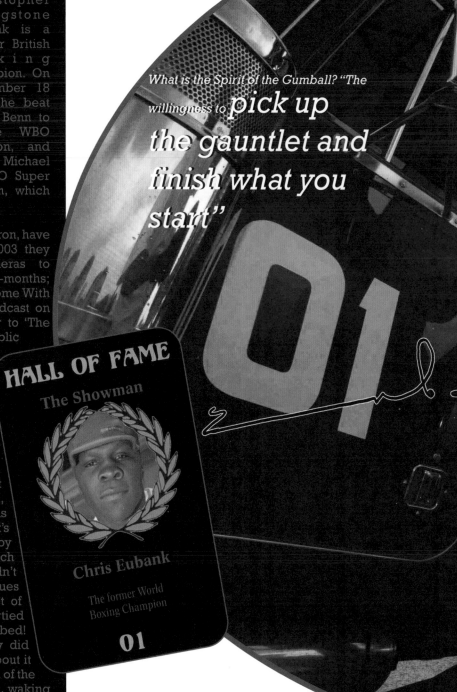

What is the Spirit of the Gumball? "The willingness to *pick up the gauntlet and finish what you start*"

HALL OF FAME
The Showman

Chris Eubank

The former World Boxing Champion

01

CHRIS EUBANK 'VS' HIS 1993 PETERBILT 379 TRUCK

PERFORMANCE	
Weight:	Super Middleweight
Wins:	45
Losses:	5
Draws:	2
Knock Outs:	24
Career:	1985-98

PERFORMANCE	
Max speed:	68 mph
0-60:	18.3 sec
Max power:	420 bhp
Miles per gallon:	5 mpg
Engine capacity:	2968 cc
Cost when new:	$300k

IN THE RING!

Many people think the Gumball is about fast cars, what made you bring the truck? *I've always liked my Peterbilt truck more than any car.*

You are a previous winner of the 'Spirit of the Gumball' – why do you think you won it? Because we completed 3000 miles in 5 days with 6 hours sleep. My wife navigated the whole time and I drove. We didn't get in one photo call on time – we were always hours behind. I think I won because no-one other that my wife and I believed that we would complete the gruelling run.

Nick Price

You are returning to the Gumball for the third time. What are your expectations? The founder [Maximillion] will be trying to trick the contestants as much as he possibly can – hence why I say finish what you start!

Many Gumballers would see the Rally as a chance to leave the wife at home and go and play with their cars. Your co-pilot each year is your wife Karron. What is the secret of a happy 6 days and 3000 miles in a truck with your wife? The best pal you have is your wife or partner. The secret is concentrating on the objective, and it brings you closer together as pals.

And finally, what are the three most important things you'll be pack-ing this year? Me, my Wife and I!

CHRIS AND KARRON. 1999 & 2004

Mike Dean

THIS YEAR CHRIS ALTERNATED BETWEEN HIS TRUCK AND BENTLEY ARNAGE

HEAVY WEIGHTS

Gumball Factor: ★★★★☆

Car 100:

Text and driver: Michael Hetelson
Co-driver: Timothy Simon

FIRST OF ITS KIND IN EUROPE

1997 Chevrolet SSR Car# 100

TRUCK ON A TRUCK

A veteran of the two US Gumball 3000 events I thought I was well prepared for the Paris-Cannes rally but the event exceeded my expectations and was an incredible test of endurance, skills, partying, and guts. The SSR is only sold in limited quantities in the USA so it is extremely rare in Europe and this one has over $140k of upgrades, it is completely custom. This extreme SSR was the ultimate babe AND police magnet with people jumping into the streets of Paris to snap photos and being stopped by police 12 times in Paris – before the rally even started! They want to make sure it was 'legal'. They did not like my anti-photo license plate which I told them was legal in the USA.

PERFORMANCE

Max speed:	224 mph in Spain (verified by digital readout and video)
0-60:	3.9 secs
Max power:	665 bhp
Miles per gallon:	16 mpg
Engine capacity:	7.0 litre
Cost when new:	$47,000, $140,000 in upgrades
Total produced:	n/a

KEEP EM ROLLIN...

Renton

GUMBALL GIVES YOU BALLS... LITERALLY

On the rally I became friends with Adrien Bro co-driver, Patrick Oldani. He is from St. Louis and huge soccer enthusiast. Patrick owned a minority sh of the St. Louis Steamers professional indoor soc team but the team was in financial difficulty and league took the team over to find new owners. Patr borrowed a video camera from me on Day 1 of the r and never gave it back. I stayed in touch with him and emailed me soccer photos and information until finally talked me into buying the team!

BLING BLING RIMS

o Wheels: Custom HRE Wheels 20" and 10" wide front 13" rear made of forged aluminum components and aerospace grade materials custom manufactured 3-piece wheels for the SSR.

o Tires: Michelin 4x4 Diamaris®

o Stereo: The hardtop convertible also sports a high-tech audio/video system. 11 speaker DVD-surround sound system. The AV system includes of components from Alpine, Zapco, DynAudio, Morel, and JL Audio.

o Other: Built in radar detection, laser detection and radar jamming. Xpel tephlon coating for the front end.

RUBBERLISHOUS

LA POLICIA - GOTTA LOVE'EM

We saw lots of police going into Spain but they just waved and gave us thumbs up. We got pulled over again in Spain leaving the Spanish Grand Prix when we were trying to get out of the crowds and jumped into a police escort procession for a government official. We talked our way out of any ticket.

Leaving Spain we got pulled over going 172 mph in France because Tim was watching the Matrix Revolutions on the DVD instead of looking out for police. The radar went off and we were actually travelling much faster. The police reduced the speed on the ticket and we paid 90 Euros, took photos, signed autographs, gave them teddy bears for their kids, and got information about the locations of all speed traps ahead.

Text: Tom Trinkle

Whether you call it a pick-up, a streetrod or, as the manufacturer prefers, a 'Super Sport Roadster', this truck oozes style. The SSR offers retro looks with a front-end reminiscent of a 1940s Chevrolet pick-up. While 19 inch wheels hold up the front end, the rear end is jacked up on 20 inch wheels, giving the vehicle a crouched and aggressive hotrod-style stance. The 5.3 litre V8 engine is quite a beast, but the pure chunkiness of the truck (weighing in at 4,700 pounds) combined with its large wheels, makes both the SSR's acceleration and steering sluggish.

Although the theme is definitely retro, the SSR is also bristling with modern features that up the luxury level such as an in-car computer and multi-adjustable seats. In addition, the two seat cab has a spectacular drop-top roof that splits into two sections when it is retracted. From a practical point of view, the SSR fails on most counts – it's heavy, slow, and space is restricted both on the inside and outside, however, it does has the instant drool factor that so many modern vehicles lack. The mean looks of this heavy Chevy will attract the attention of even the most eccentric of fellow Gumballers.

MADE IT TO CANNES

SAFETY COMES FIRST!

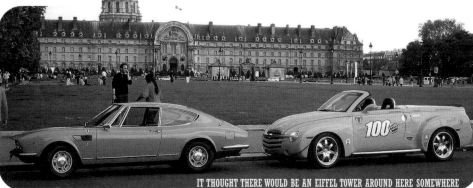
IT THOUGHT THERE WOULD BE AN EIFFEL TOWER AROUND HERE SOMEWHERE

ENGINE PACKAGE:
Custom Chevy 410 CID LS1, LS6 package High Compression Version

o Engine removal, inspection and disassembly

o Custom 7.0 L steel block preparation

o CNC porting & polishing of cylinder heads

o BPP valve springs and valve spring retainers

o Stainless steel intake/exhaust valves

o 3 angle valve job, checking of spring tensions and heights

o Custom designed BPP

hydraulic roller camshaft

o Custom forged aluminum pistons – 11.5:1 comp

o Custom forged steel crankshaft & billet steel connecting rods

o Computer balanced rotating assembly

o Reassembly of the engine

o Professional installation, testing and tuning

o Chassis dyno testing after installation

o Original engine reused for cores

o 44lb Injectors

o Custom Headers

o Custom Exhaust dual system

o Custom Ram Induction System

o Custom Heavy Duty Dual Radiator

o Custom racing transmission and gear box

o Custom shocks and springs suspension

T THIS BEAST ON THE ROAD

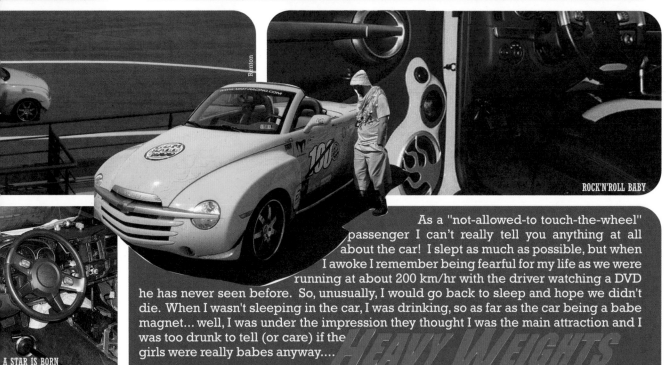
Renton
ROCK'N'ROLL BABY

As a "not-allowed-to touch-the-wheel" passenger I can't really tell you anything at all about the car! I slept as much as possible, but when I awoke I remember being fearful for my life as we were running at about 200 km/hr with the driver watching a DVD he has never seen before. So, unusually, I would go back to sleep and hope we didn't die. When I wasn't sleeping in the car, I was drinking, so as far as the car being a babe magnet... well, I was under the impression they thought I was the main attraction and I was too drunk to tell (or care) if the girls were really babes anyway....

A STAR IS BORN

HEAVY WEIGHTS

GOOD PUBLICITY SHOT FOR 'MOHAMMED'S AUTO FIX'

Dan Anslow

K & VAN RESCUE

**ANCIENT MEDINA,
FES EL-JDID, MOROCCO**

CHECKPOINT:

Moroccan
drive-thru

Enjoy a true
Moroccan lunch hour
experience and take a few
moments to step into the
maze of alleyways and buy a
Kaftan and some magic
slippers!

Fact of the day:
From this great city Fassis
scholars introduced
astronomy and medicine to
the West, and translated Plato
and Aristotle.

Today, Fez still rules
the country spiritually if not
politically, as it plays out an
incredible human drama of life
as it must have been many
hundreds of years ago.

MY04 GT2

Nick Melton

Style Tip: Men still wear
fezes in Fez,
and so should you!

Learn to say: "Follow me my
friend" or "Balek!!!" (Out of
the way!)

It wasn't hard to imagine we'd
gone back in time. Fez is one of
the world's oldest continuously
inhabited cities, dating back to the
early ninth century.

"I'M NOT A PORSCHE MAN MYSELF,
BUT NICE RIMS MATE"

Mileage: **295**

Hours on road: **5 - 7**

Total mileage: **1854**

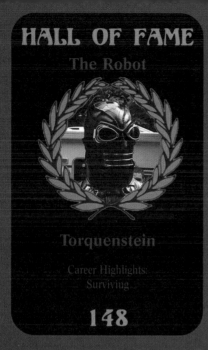

HALL OF FAME
The Robot

Torquenstein

Career Highlights:
Surviving

148

THE ROBOT

First name please:
Torquenstein.

Home town:
Born and raised by rebels in icy Siberia.

Career highlights?
Escaped from the government at fifteen. Tortured in the deadly prisons of China. Abolished 29 racers in five days during my first race. Lost almost all my limbs in subsequent car races and crashes.

If you had to say, what would be you your best and worst moments on the Gumball?
Best moment–Receiving recognition at the awards ceremony "Safety First." Worst–The first leg–1000 miles, two days without sleep and not being able to go faster in France because of the stinking rain!!! The Hennessey Venom does not handle all that well in the rain at high speeds.

What would your advice be to other motor-drivers considering the Gumball 3000 as their spring rally?
Nothing will prepare you for the "thrill" of Gumball! NEVER give up!! NEVER Surrender!!

Did you find the Spirit of the Gumball?
Yes I did. I made it to the finish line no matter what!! Also if you knew John and Gary [2CV boys]......you would know the spirit of the Gumball. They definitely have it!!

DO YOU HAVE THE GUTS TO LOOK AT TORQUENSTEIN...

TORQUENSTEIN'S ULTIMATE RACING MACHINE:

THE HENNESSEY VENOM 650R PERFORMANCE
- 700 BHP
- 0-60 in 2.99 Sec!
- 1/4 mile: 10.76 @ 132 mph
- v10
- Convertible
- Red

TORQUENSTEIN'S LIFE SAVING VEHICLE:

2003 HUMMER H2 SPORT UTILITY PERFORMANCE
- E.R.S.V / Emergency Road Side Vehicle
- Transportation vehicle for Torquenstein's Pit Crew & Science Team
- Thermal night vision camera
- Cool YAK skull on grill
- Yellow

Illustrations and layout: Matt Delahunt

THE LEGEND OF

HALF MAN HALF MACHINE   **RACING IS HIS LIFE'S MISSION**

TORQUENSTEIN

Born, Thorn 'Tork' Severniak, the only sibling of political prisoners captured by the Red Army. Tork grew up hearing his father's stories about the rallies he used to participate in, and he used to say, "one day Tork, you will be a real race-car driver." Often, as a child, he dreamt of winning many big car race's.

Years later in a planned escape, Tork raced through the tundra for 5 days driving a stolen government-owned Volga, but upon reaching Beijing he was imprisoned suspected of being one of Stalin's spies. After months of life-and-death battles in the Chinese prison he was selected to take part in a car race organized in honour of the Great Chinese ruler Mao Tse-Tung, along with 29 other prisoners of war. It was a race of life and death, and winning the race was the only way to get out of it alive!

Tork won this race and his freedom, running over all 29 of his rivals in the process. This freedom cost him his left eye and his left hand, up to the shoulder. The loss of body parts desensitized his left side completely and made the right half of his body stronger. From a prisoner he quickly became a renowned race car driver, but the many crashes started to take their toll and Torque's facial features had to be covered by a leather mask and numerous mechanical additions and alterations to his body made it hard to think of him as human. The constantly changing and evolving Tork became known as "Torquenstein," the Steel Monster.

Today, Torquenstein is still winning the maddest, deadliest races in the world, and is one of the drivers who took part in the Gumball in May 2004 with his 700 HP Hennessey Venom 650R.

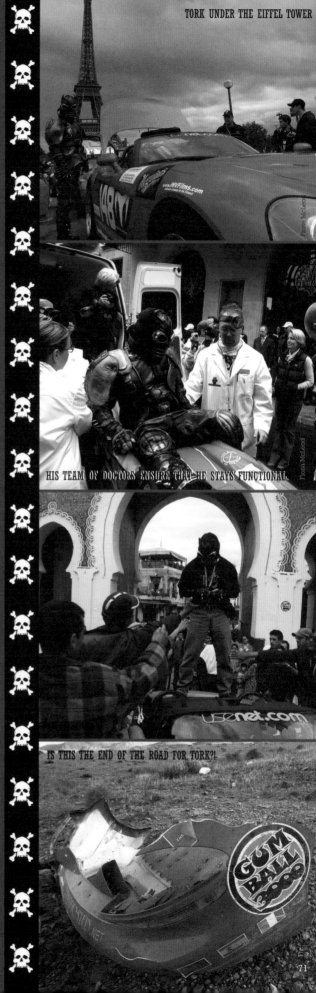

TORK UNDER THE EIFFEL TOWER

HIS TEAM OF DOCTORS ENSURE THAT HE STAYS FUNCTIONAL.

IS THIS THE END OF THE ROAD FOR TORK?!

DESTINATION:
Transmediterrania Ferry

PORT OF NADOR, MOROCCO
8th MAY, 2004

The ferry MUST depart at 10 PM so this leg of the rally is where your 'map reader' has to pay attention! No rest for the wicked!!

Tip: As the road narrows into two-way traffic, the 'real' Moroccan driving experience begins. Keep your speed down and watch out for donkeys, shepherds with sheep, camels and stray dogs - especially when entering small towns. If you get lost, ask, and give Gumball stickers plentifully, you'll find people really helpful!

SUPERCART RECOVERY
SERVICE FOLLOWS THE ACTION!

الوقاية المدنية

WAVE TO MAX!

Mileage: **199**

Hours on road: **3-5**

Total mileage: **2053**

AND THE SUPERCART TAKES THE LEAD!

Frederike Helwig

The Ai-Ya Boys

Fiat Ducato 2.3 Turbo luxury Campervan (Winnebago)

Welcome to Planet Ai-Ya
no one is safe...

Their career highlights include "fake sneezing on pedestrians in Hong Kong during the SARS epidemic", MTV Asia favourites, The Aiya Boys, are the ultimate urban assault team, armed with cameras and full of insane ideas, no one is safe...

Performance

Max speed (mph) :	*70 on a flat road, 95 going down hill when we really pushed it.*
0-60 (seconds):	*We can't really count that high*
Max power (bhp):	*Power? Try lack of power!*
Miles per gallon:	*Huh?*
Engine capacity:	*2300cc*
Cost when new:	*People pay for these things?*
Total produced:	*The less the better!*

Jacob Mense aka Pok Guy
THE PRODUCER

Fight Specialty
The power of being the producer!
(Does it impress the ladies?)
Don't really care (I'm gay)

Storyline: Gumball 3000 rally from the skewed point of view of 13 people trapped in a Motorhome licensed to carry only 6 passengers for however many days we were stuck in there.
(Catch all the action on MTV and a special 'Ai-Ya Rock the Gumball' film later this year).

Interview with producer Jacob Mense:
Car driven in Gumball?
Fiat Ducato 2.3 Turbo luxury Campervan.

Turbo???? I think they forgot to put in the Turbo.

Any special mod's?
13 people and 500 lbs. of luggage. 50 lbs. of human excrement in a toilet, which we had no idea how to drain. We broke every door handle and light switch, not to mention the bathroom door, which we finally had to tape shut to prevent us from suffocating on the

James McNaught

Roye Segal aka Charlie Hustle
DIRECTOR & co-PRODUCER

Fight Specialty **Get the shot and get the f**k out**
(Does it impress the ladies?)
Depends on the angle

David Ismalone aka
MAS JOG
Muay Thai World Champion

Fight Specialty
MuayThai Kick yo ass style
(Does it impress the ladies?)
Only the lady-boys

Joshua Lee
SHOW co-HOST
Hapkido Champion

Fight Specialty **Hapkido**
(Does it impress the ladies?)
The big rough ones

foul stench. Do spray paint cou as a specia modification? Where did yo get the motor home from? W got it fro another Gumba participant.

THE DRIVER
Oil the Arab

Paul Lowey- Production Manager
Henry Chung- Cameraman
Ah Long- Edison's assistant

Anthony- Given to us by Kimble because he didn't have enough room in his car...

Shane- before he rode with us.

Anthony with 'Initiation Haircut' and after being locked in the toilet for 6 hours...

...cars that we stopped to help. We ended up picking up the drivers or taking a piece of their car to the finish.

"I know everyplace, everything"

" Imagine a race car driver in a motorhome thinking that it was a Ferarri."

EBAGO AT THE START LINE

Syan... MCE

MADE IN HONG KONG

Rapper, Graffiti Artist and philosopher, Syan aka MC Yan, along with his band LMF (Lazy Mutha F**kas), virtually invented Canto-Rap in Hong Kong. He's worked with the notorious DJ Krush and appeared in an international Nike campaign featuring him bombing the streets of Japan. He's spawned a popular MC Yan action figure.

Edison Chen is a massive Hong Kong Star and idol. This year he appears in the movies Infernal Affairs and Twins Effect.

The most outrageous thing he's ever done? "Go to Gumball wid the Aiya Crew!"

How did you all get on in the van?
Get on? Get on what? 13 guys...what is there to get on? The first day was exciting until Edison's assistant, who doesn't read or speak any English, drove us 300 Kilometers off course. That was the last time he drove!

You should have seen his face when he first saw it covered in grafitti! Arrghh!! Thank God he didn't speak much English. So as compensation I offered to spray paint his company website on the van (product placement) and he was cool with it.

THE RAPPER
MC Yan

Fight Specialty
Aiiiiyaaa!!

Okay then.. Tips on how to stay stylish at the Gumball?
Bomb my own car...

THE PAIN GUY
Min Yoo

Fight Specialty Tae Kwon Do
(Does it impress the ladies?)
not since the sixth grade

WARSROBE
Jeff Lowey aka Jack Lando

Fight Specialty
Ralph Macchio Swan Kick
(Does it impress the ladies?)
Only my grandmother

HONG KONG SUPERSTAR
Edison Chen

Fight Specialty Tiger Style
(Does it impress the ladies?)
Dnn need to fight to impress the ladies

You all arrived a day late in Cannes.. what happened?

We think you lost us because we were 13 demented lunatics averaging 70 km/h in a Fiat "Luxury" Motorhome built for 6 with an onboard toilet carrying way more shit than it should, having no maps whatsoever because our driver, Oil The Arab, said, "I know everyplace everything," but he knew no place nothing - except how to honk and whistle at every girl in every goddamn car that flew past – and believe us, many did – because none of us noticed that The Arab was going sideways for his co-pilot; MC Yan was in a hypnotic hip-hop trance and Jacob was on the phone the whole f***ing time talking to god-knows-who while Josh was waxing Anthony's chest-hair with duct tape next to Mad Dog, who was trying to yank Paul's front teeth out with a rusty plier (he had good grip, but no leverage!!) while distracted by Min who was poised - feet up, spread eagle - with a lighter between his legs, hoping to "set one off for real this time", praying and spluttering on the hot beans force-fed to him by Lando who was bringing them to a gentle boil on the stove while Edison slept the sleep of angels and Hustle had the lens cap on and filmed none of it. But, we're not sure.

And what happened to the Winnebego?

None of us actually returned the motorhome. It was kind of abandoned in Paris after the Gumball for a few days, then it broke down at a gas station on the way back to Germany, then it was left there for a couple of days, then it was brought back to Paris to see what was wrong with it, then it was left there again for a couple of days, then it was driven to Munich by some friends where it was left on the street with the keys in it for a couple of days, then the owners found it! They were NOT happy.....

アイーヤ月!
COLOUR FUN

Afro Ninjas dancing in Morocco with Diva Kym Mazelle and MC Ninja Yan

Afro Ninjas with Bucky in Morocco

Colour fun in Morocco with the Ai-YA boys!!! Gather together anthing you can find that makes a mark and colour in your own 'grafitti' Winnebego!

Shane's initiation - shaving anthony's eyebrows

Lando sunbathing in Barcelona

Mad Dog and Josh disguised as engineers on the ferry back from Morocco-watch the movie to see what they did

Shane's really having fun with us

Badass Badminton in Cannes

Chicken wok boarding in Morocco

Oil the Driver crying over broken Ferarri

What happened to Shane?

En route to rejoin the Rally after being stuck in Morocoo, Maximillion steps off his flight and into a bar in Madrid, Spain. There he finds Gumballer Shane intoxicated at the bar.. he'd been there since the day before, having gotten lost on his way to Barcelona. (They both make it to the finish line.)

THE AL-YA BOYS CATCH THE THIEF WHO STOLE THEIR COLOURS!!

Main photo: Rophon. Photos this page and previous pages: Al-Ya Boys; Alex Roy, Fly James McNaught

Ruben Fleischer arrived in Paris a day before the rally began having been commissioned to direct a docufilm of the event, but with no idea what the Gumball was all about.

6 days later and Ruben was a fully committed Gumballer for life. His film follows the antics and experiences of a handful of drivers, and has all the stylish, quirky and raw quality that has given rise to Rubens reputation as one of Hollywood's hottest new talents.

Ruben cut his teeth as assistant director on 'Chuck & Buck' and 'The Good Girl', then spent the last two years directing music videos, short films and commercials for the likes of Gold Chains, Dizzee Rascal, Vladivar Vodka, and KFC.

Although he admits he didn't originally set out to be a director, because *"it seemed unattainable, and almost cliche, because there are so many young kids in LA who fancy themselves directors, and I didn't want to be just another!"* But after kicking around Hollywood in various assistant jobs, working 16 hour days six days a week for $200/week, he learned everything there was to know about production and filmmaking.

Car driven in Gumball?
VW Toureg and Mercedes SUV
Any special modifications? Full of film equipment!
You are making a feature length film about this year's Gumball Rally. What's your own favourite car related movie? I hate to be obvious, but I got to go with Cannonball Run. It's the template for what we tried to do, and what's funny is that the personalities in this year's Gumball eclipsed those in the movie.
How many cameras and crew did you have? We had about nine cameras of all different shapes and sizes to cover all different angles and situations.

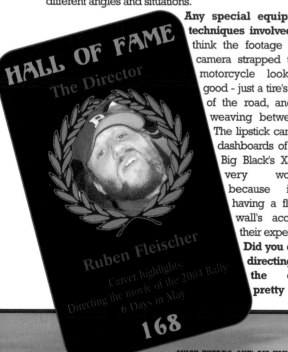

HALL OF FAME
The Director

Ruben Fleischer
Career highlights:
Directing the movie of the 2004 Rally-
6 Days in May

168

Any special equipment or techniques involved? Well, I think the footage from the camera strapped to Karta's motorcycle looks really good - just a tire's eye view of the road, and all the weaving between cars. The lipstick cams on the dashboards of Rob and Big Black's X5 proved very worthwhile, because it's like having a fly on the wall's access into their experience.
Did you do lots of directing or did the cameras pretty much

roll and the stories tell themselves? I just tried to be in the right place at the right time, so I could capture the most dramatic moments - although it was a huge challenge given the inherent unpredictability of Gumball. I think my most important decision was made in the teams I chose to follow. Selecting 7 of the 192 cars was a challenge, particularly having known nothing about any of them before the rally started.
How did the project compare to your previous work? It's absolutely unique, as I have never been a part of any road rally or endurance test of this scale. While all the other Gumballers were just trying to drive and have fun, we had to actually work while driving the same rigorous route that they took.
Who were the most interesting, inspiring characters you came across? Pretty much everyone in a different way, whether it be 'the-little-engine-that-could' of the 2CV, or the larger than life personality of Kim Schmitz, or the comedy duo that is Rob & Big Black.
Your favorite quote from the film? "Payback's a b*tch!" - Big Black after just having mooned a Moroccan.
What was your worst moment on the Gumball? I think when I crashed into a tollbooth, thereby waking the three sleeping people in my car who proceeded to yell at me for the rest of the trip, and prohibited me from any further driving.
What was your best moment on the Gumball?
Going faster than I ever have (165mph) and still getting passed by loads of cars.
Top 3 essential items to bring on the Gumball?
A camera, a crew, and a Big Black.
What, to you, is the Spirit of the Gumball?
A willingness to make the most of the experience. Dropping your guard, and just being in the moment, to the fullest, at all times. Gumball is like a vacuum, and the Spirit of the Gumball is the feeling that pervades everyone while you exist in that vacuum.
Sum up your **Gumball 3000 experience in one word?** Footage!

QUICK THERE'S ONE! DID YOU GET IT?!

6 Days in May
.....a film by ruben fleischer

A GUMBALL 3000 FILM

'6 DAYS IN MAY' WILL BE RELEASED ON DVD IN THE SPRING OF 2005

6 DAYS IN MAY

EN FLEISCHER

PRODUCTION '6 DAYS IN MAY' EXECUTIVE PRODUCERS: MAXIMILLION COOPER
ASSISTANT EDITOR JUSTIN BARHAM MUSIC SUPERVISOR DAVE FREEMAN
BY RUBEN FLEISCHER THE GUMBALL 3000 RALLY IS A
...PER
...rocco's Chief of Security

Sequence: Dan Anslow

LONE RIDER- KARTA'S
MOTORCYCLE DIARIES

CHECKPOINT:
Barcelona Grand Prix

CIRCUIT DE CATALUNYA
SPAIN, 9 MAY 2004
Checkpoint open:11am - 2pm

During the race, we've got a proper 'F1 style' lunch of Hot Dogs and Burgers in the Gumballers car park area. Don't say we don't look after you guys!

Style Tip: Ear plugs will look great here

Learn to say: It was a busy day. After an electrical problem in the morning, I had to abort one run when I came across a big puff of smoke in the tunnel and thought there was oil on the track. Then on one run, I had a traffic problem with Juan-Pablo, which is just down to the nature of this track and after my second run, I also picked up something in my eye" (Just another day on the Gumball!)?

The Gumball 3000 Grandstand was on the start line straight, a prime location to see lots of action!

come on Jenson!

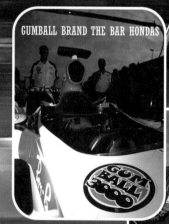

GUMBALL BRAND THE BAR HONDAS

COME ON GIRLS YOU CAN DO BETTER THAN THAT!

Mileage: 494
Hours on road: 5-8
Total mileage: 2547

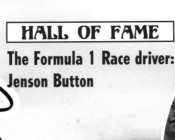

HALL OF FAME

The Formula 1 Race driver: Jenson Button

Born: Somerset, England, lives in Monaco.

Have you ever done any long-distance Rally driving? *No. The furthest I have ever driven was from Mercedes AMG in Germany to England when I picked up my new SL55 AMG.*

Would you consider doing the Gumball in the future? *I would definitely consider doing the Gumball in the future, but I am not sure whether I would be permitted to participate while I am still driving in F1. I would love to do it while I am still in F1, but we'll see.*

Would it be to race or party? *I think a bit of both. Obviously I would love to play around with some great cars throughout the rally and to do it with some cool people.*

Who would be your dream co-driver? *Louise, my fiancée, or one of my best friends.*

Would you let Cameron Diaz and the rest of the Angels overtake you to be polite? *No, but I would let them drive with me in the same car.*

What's your favorite thing to do in a car? *Apart from the obvious?! I love to drive fast and I am extremely fortunate that I get to do it for a living.*

What's your Best car stunt ever? *Doing donuts in a Formula 1 car in Regent Street in London.*

A lot of people say that when they go on the Gumball it wasn't what they expected. Do you think you know what you're in for? *I've seen the film so I have some idea of what I'm in for.*

How many marks out of 10 would you give the Gumball Movie from last year? *8/10 – because I wasn't in it!*

What's the craziest Gumball story you've heard? *The craziest Gumball story was probably the one about the dude in the Viper who was being chased by the police and didn't stop. He just kept going. After losing the police, I think he then left his car hidden for a few hours in a forest and waited for the police to leave. He was in the Gumball film and looked a bit of a nutter!*

At just twenty years old, Jenson Button was the youngest driver on the grid for the 2000 season, impressing everyone with his coolness and race pace. Following a season with Benetton, he signed a deal with BAR Honda in 2003, and has continued to impress ever since. He currently sits third in the Drivers World Championship, having brought BAR Honda up the ranks to sit proudly just behind Ferrari in the Constructors Championship.

As the 'superstar' of Formula One with undeniable talent, could the 2005 season prove to be his Championship winning year?

GUMBALL 3000 GIVES YOU BALLS

1 A Lamborghini overta[kes] Almeria's mayor's car, the cops decide th[ey] should get on the ca[se]. They stop Gumballers a[nd] tell them 'no more than 1[...] mph please' half an ho[ur] later they catch some gu[y] doing 200mph and deci[de] to stop everyone and issu[e] tickets.

2 Word gets out and the Gumballers start calling their friends who are behind, the warning rings the same: "Cops are waiting at the toll, pulling over every single car that has Gumball stickers. And automatically issuing a 350 Euro fine."

Alexander Roy, winner of last yea[rs] Spirit of the Gumball Award. Last year he was NYPD, this year [he] had a different tailored police ou[tfit] for every day of the rally!

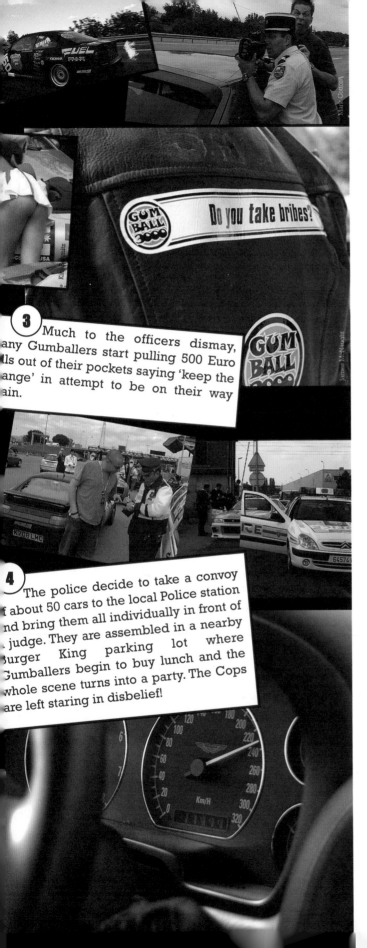

Car 145:

Text and driver: Rob Kenworthy (aka Lonman)
Co-driver: Aldo Riti

What car did you drive on the Gumball?
Porsche GT2. (1 CPU)
How did it perform?
Faultless. It's a Porsche.
What was your top speed?
It's unbelievable! So I'd rather not say.
Did anything break on the car?
Yes, a Donkey's nose in Morocco. It didn't stop, look and listen before crossing. (Only joking!)
What was the best moment on the Gumball?
Getting out after 2 days in solitary. I was on a hunger strike and they had a Burger King next to the Tarragona Police HQ.
What was your worst moment on the Gumball?
Sitting in a cell realising that there were great parties going on in Barcelona and Cannes, and not being part of it all. Then a few days later being released and just driving home...Gumball over. We'll slow down next year!
Did you like driving in Morocco?
Yes. An unbelievable experience. The people were amongst the nicest I've ever met. The landscape was spectacular and the roads were fast. I think we won 3 out of the 4 stages in Morocco, just fast, flat out fun everywhere.
Tell me a little story about your Gumball experience?
You really have to do a Gumball to appreciate what it's all about. To drive fast cars across continents, party hard every night, stay in top hotels, meet new friends. Is that not what all boys dream of???
Marks out of 10 for this years experience?
10.
Marks out of 10 for your cars performance?
9. The yellow Enzo overtook me at 220mph in Morocco, we were doing well over 200mph at the time. Then he broke down. It was the first time I've been overtaken on the Gumball in 3 years, next year same car, longer 6th gear and even more noise and power.

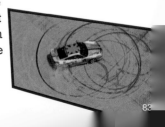

3 Much to the officers dismay, many Gumballers start pulling 500 Euro bills out of their pockets saying 'keep the change' in attempt to be on their way again.

4 The police decide to take a convoy of about 50 cars to the local Police station and bring them all individually in front of a judge. They are assembled in a nearby Burger King parking lot where Gumballers begin to buy lunch and the whole scene turns into a party. The Cops are left staring in disbelief!

GUMBaLL 3000 &

GIVES you BALLS

The famous train robber Bruce Reynolds did the Gumball in 2000 in a Bentley Azur

You have been quoted as saying the Gumball was your greatest adventure?
Bruce: The gumball was the latest great adventure in a life of great adventure!
The first time that I drove the route from Spain to London was in 1961 returnin
from running with the bulls at Pamplona, in my soon to be written o
Austin Healey! Now many years later, whilst driving in the company
Lamborghini's, it occurred to me that the Gumball could I
interpreted as the motoring equivalent of Pamplona, ('the festiv
of San Fermin') - to do it either one, or both indicates
propensity for lunacy!

What was your greatest moment?
Bruce: Bilbao to Cannes in time for the finale of the Cann
Film Festival and staying at the Hotel Martinez and 'twistir
the night away' on the Gumball yacht.

Did you have any encounters with the police?
Bruce: Only at country borders where we were oft
stopped. At one point our bags were searched but lucki
they didn't recognise me or find my private stash.

Can you sum up the Gumball in one word?
Bruce: No, but I can say it in three, 'its the bol**cks!'

Anything you'd like to add?
Bruce: Great route, great hotels, great food, great cars, gre
camaraderie, Maximillion is a great host!

GUMBALL PROMISE: BUY A GUMBALL GIVES YOU BALLS T-SHIRT AND GUMBALL WILL DONATE £1 TO THE EVERYMAN CHARITY.

GREAT TRAIN ROBBER, BRUCE REYNOLDS, WANTING TO BE HIMSELF

BRUCE ON THE GUMBALL 2000

KEEP YOUR EYE ON THE BALL!!!

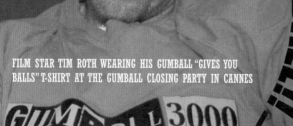

FILM STAR TIM ROTH WEARING HIS GUMBALL "GIVES YOU BALLS" T-SHIRT AT THE GUMBALL CLOSING PARTY IN CANNES

JUST WHAT IS TESTICULAR CANCER?

Testicular cancer is a malignant tumour that develops fror
cells within the testes – or "balls". It is the most commo
cancer in men between the ages of 20 and 35 and th
incidence of testicular cancer has risen by 70 per cer
over the last 20 years. The causes of the increase are
unknown.

SYMPTOMS

Testicular cancer symptoms:
* a lump in either testicle
* enlargement of a testicle
* a heavy feeling in the scrotum
* a dull ache in the abdomen, groin or scrotum
* a sudden collection of fluid in the scrotum
* growth or tenderness of the upper chest
Most lumps are benign but changes in size, shape o
weight should be checked by your doctor.

TREATMENT AND SURVIVAL

Thanks to the treatment Everyman discovered, up t
96% of cases of testicular cancer can be cured if th
diagnosis is at an early stage. Regular self-examinatio
of testicles is important and can help with early detectio
and hence chances of survival.

For further information please contact: Tel: 020 7153 5297 or 0800 731 9468
Fax: 020 7970 6018
E-mail: everyman@icr.ac.uk

Horse Power
Richard Dunwoody MBE

HALL OF FAME
The Jockey

Richard Dunwoody
2003 Volvo V70R

79

RICHARD DUNWOODY BROKE ALL RECORDS AS THE MOST SUCCESSFUL JUMP JOCKEY IN HISTORY. IN 2004 HE DID THE GUMBALL.

Home town:
Belfast, Ireland.

Career highlights: Winning Grand National in '86 and '94, Champion National Hunt Jockey in Britain 93-95.

You drove a Volvo V70R. Why?
Co-driver Clement Wilson picked it up from Volvo PR office. Volvo was keen to be compared to all the supercars on the Rally.

Any special modifications? Integrated child seat.

Did you give your car a cool, encouraging horse name, like 'Very Promising' or 'Desert Orchid'? Jess!

Your peers used to call you 'The Prince'. So what are your supreme, pimping Gumball style tips? We wore suits provided by Cordings of Piccadilly.

What's your favourite car related movie? Bullit, Grand Prix.

'Car movies' compared to 'horse movies'? Seabiscuit was so good, by far the best horse movie!

Why did you take up motor racing and rallying? I like competing and speed.

What do you think drives people to win? For me it's competition. I don't like loosing. And a fear of failure.

You are known for being a brilliant inspirational speaker, what were your words of encouragement to others during the Rally? My first words to Clement after the wing accident were, (accent suddenly becomes VERY Irish), "You f***in eejit!"

3 reasons cars are better than horses? They have brakes, they don't kick (though some people say they can bite you), no mucking out!

Who from history would be your dream Gumball co-driver? Charlie's Angels (old or new team, no preference).

What was your worst moment on the Gumball? Heading off the road straight into a signpost wondering how far it was concreted into the ground. Fortunately it hadn't been as it was by my side!

Best moment on the Gumball? Undertaking the black Lamborghini which was trying to overtake the Merc AMG Estate.

What, to you, is the Spirit of the Gumball? Whatever it is, the Moroccan police had it!

Finally, what's the most outrageous thing you've ever done? As this is a family publication...travelling 350 miles to the magnetic North Pole last year – hoping to go to the Geographic in 2005!

Please sum up your Gumball 3000 experience in one word? Mind blowing!

HOTEL REY JUAN CARLOS
BARCELONA, SPAIN
9 MAY 2004

Fiona McLeod

IT'S NOT EVERY DAY BAR-HONDA LOAN AN F1 CAR
TO THE GUMBALL!

Mileage: **24**   Hours on road: **1**   Total mileage: **2571**

Chec
the
freshen
and then
the red car
dinner in
Garden Mar
After dinner, dan
night away at the

IG BROTHER'S ALWAYS WATCHING

nown to everyone the Hotels were making Gumball films too. Here, Spillie in 'Gumball Spa 01'. They were kind enough to send stills to ball HQ a week after the Rally. Look out for the nball Spa 01 *Uncut*' and presumably we expect some sequels...

iball Spa 01 Film:

Rey Juan CCTV Footage

FUN

HALL OF FAME
The Big Brother Winner

Spillie
2004 Hummer H2
12

Spillie

'S WIFE IS SHE SPILLIE?

1969 Shelby Mustang GT350

This is what happened back in the 1960s when Ford asked the top racing car driver in America to add a few special touches to its already very special Mustang. The car's sporty image has proved a runaway success with American boy racers since its launch in 1964. With a lengthened hood, chrome grille and bumpers, and the famous wild horse insignia, this American classic dripped with style. Appearances in the James Bond movies Thunderball and Goldfinger helped to ensure the car's legendary status.

In 1965, Ford teamed up with Carroll Shelby, American racing hero and head of Shelby American cars, to produce the Shelby Mustang GT 350. On the surface it looked similar to a regular Mustang but lurking under the bonnet was Ford's 4,738 cc small-block V8 engine, giving it a top speed of about 150 mph, while the front suspension was also modified to give it more of a neutral ride. The combination of Ford's classic design and Shelby's racing legacy made this Mustang one of the original boy racer dream cars.

GT500E "GONE IN 60 SECONDS"

Nick Pride

SHELBY MUSTANG GT500 "ELEANOR"

Driver: Matk Biestman, Co-driver Valli Robert

The Shelby Mustang GT500E "Eleanor" is genuinely famous, having starred alongside Nicolas Cage in the film Gone In Sixty Seconds, released in 2000. In the film, Cage is an ex-master car thief who has to come out of retirement to pull off an audacious heist of 50 rare classic cars and supercars to save his brother's life. This Shelby Mustang is the last car he steals and it gets seriously mashed up in the final chase scene.

PERFORMANCE

Text & Driver: Matt Treadwell
Co-driver: Alistair Robertson

Max speed:	116 mph
0-60:	5 ish secs
Max power:	300 bhp
Miles per gallon:	You dont want to know
Engine capacity:	5500 cc
Cost when new:	$3500
Total produced:	935
Modifications:	A self-stopping engine when wet and/or dark. Comatose copilot

The Shelby was very comfortable but LOUD, although, that didn't stop Al from getting a nice view of the inside of his eyelids from Murcia to Cannes. It was great to drive but a bit of a whale – a nightmare on the track. The only real problem was the lack of lights and the tendency to break down in the rain. Also having to fill up every hour was a bit of a pain in the arse. It got lots of attention, as it should have. It's a beautiful car. Al proved to be more of a babe magnet than the car. No one was more surprised than I!

AL... BABEMAGNET APPARENTLY...

What's in the Engine? WHERE'S THE MUSTANG?

FROM DUST TILL DAWN

Matt Treadwell

BOY RACERS

FIRE STARTER, TWISTED FIRE STARTER

1996 NISSAN SKYLINE GTR V-SPEC R33

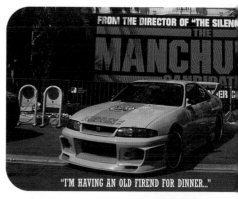

"I'M HAVING AN OLD FIREND FOR DINNER..."

The Nissan Skyline R33 GT-R it is at the top end of this category of Gumballers. It may not be as distinct as other cars in the rally but what the Skyline lacks in looks it makes up for in sophisticated Japanese technology on the inside. The ATTESA-ETS (Advanced Total Traction Engineering System for All-Electronic Torque Split) system that controls the all-wheel drive set-up usually sends power to the rear wheels but can send up to 50% of the torque to the front wheels, allowing the driver to execute drifts at high speed. The Skyline used in the Gumball is a highly modified V-Spec version with an even more advanced ATTESA-ETS system as well as stiffer and lower suspension. This is all combined with great steering courtesy of Nissan's Super-HICAS all-wheel steering system.

The Skyline R33 GT-R, first launched in 1995, is more of a useable, everyday sportscar than its predecessors, with practical features such as a larger boot and airbags. However, there's no getting away from the fact that this seriously desirable beast still has bucket seats as standard and will have most boy racers' mouths frothing with drool.

AAAAHHHH

I LOOK SO GOOD I MAKE MYSELF JEALOUS

PERFORMANCE

Text & Driver: Sona & Dan - Renton - Lewis

Max speed:	Well off the clock (stops counting at 180mph)
0-60:	3.8 sec
Max power:	650 bhp
Miles per gallon:	13 mpg
Engine capacity:	2.6 ltr
Cost when new:	£50,000 (for standard car)
Total produced:	16,289 (includes nonV-Spec models)
Modifications:	DoLuck and Jun bodykit, Racing Hart rims

with Pirelli rubber, uprated AP acing brakes all round, TEIN Flex suspension, Abbey Motorsport/Blitz engine kicking out over 650bhp

THE ULTIMATE HONEYMOON

NO PLACE LIKE HOME

EVEN THE RACE TRACKS MATCH US

Text: Tom Trinkle,

I HAVE TO FIND IT OR THAT'S IT

HEY DUDE...YOU LEFT HALF YOUR TYRE OVER THERE.

WE THOUGHT YOU SAID GO FASTER

THE ENGINE WAS MAPPED TO RUN ON SUPER UNLEADED, BUT THAT'S NOT AVAILABLE IN MOROCCO SO WE HAD TO TURN THE TURBO BOOST DOWN TO AVOID MELTING THE PISTONS. THAT MEANT WE WERE ABOUT 150BHP DOWN.

D THIS BABY REALLY IS...

SURE YOU DON'T KNOW WHERE THEY SELL SUPER UNLEADED?

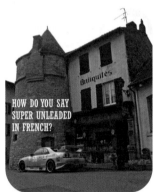

HOW DO YOU SAY SUPER UNLEADED IN FRENCH?

WE LOVED THE ROAD AND THE ROAD LOVED US RIGHT BACK

MAYBE THIS IS WHERE I PUT IT

From the Road
Driver: Renton

I'm mad about cars, so when my girlfriend (now wife) suggested we did the Gumball for our honeymoon I didn't need asking twice! I work for a modified car magazine so I was lucky enough to have a few high performance cars to choose from. I went for the Skyline, because it's safe, reliable and huge, so Sona could bring as many pairs of shoes as she wanted! But the best bit is under the bonnet: a highly tuned, turbocharged six-pot engine putting the power down through an active 4WD transmission. It turned out to be a fantastic Gumball tool, running faultlessly. The only area the Skyline fell down on was fuel economy. We had to stop a total of 23 times over the six-day drive! So if we do it again next year I'll probably modify the boot into a giant fuel tank…

BOY RACERS

Gumball Factor: ★★★★☆

Mean Mud Eating

WHEN YOU COME HOME - HAVE A SHOWER

WX53 HYF

Frederike Helwig

Dan Anslow

2004 Mitsubishi Lancer Evolution VIII FQ300

With its incredible Active Centre Differential system that ensures grip on even the loosest surfaces, the Evo allows the most ham-fisted driver to tear round bends like a pro. The car's extensive use in the World Rally Championship means it can stand up to the most brutal conditions while also delivering turbo-charged power to all four wheels. The Evo has an impressive racing pedigree but it has the body of a four-door saloon which is advantageous on the lengthy Gumball Rally when practicality and comfort are highly appreciated by drivers. The enormous spoiler bolted to the boot, however, does attract attention and is a huge giveaway to any passing cops that the Evo has the ability to obliterate speed limits.

Text: Tom Trinkle

PERFORMANCE

Text & Driver: Yorgo Tloupas
Co-driver: Julia Martens & Frederike Helwig

Max speed:	157mph supposedly (but we did a steady 175mph on the third day)
0-60:	4.8 estimated
Max power:	305.4 bhp
Miles per gallon:	you don't want to know
Engine capacity:	1997 cc
Cost when new:	£28,999 OTR + £280 if metallic paint
Total produced:	500-600 to be produced at present

If it wasn't for it's thirstiness, the EVO would probably be the ultimate Gumball vehicle: fast but stable on all types of roads, discreet enough not to attract Police attention, but still sufficiently cool to generate cheers from the crowds of car freaks gathered at the checkpoints, sporty and loud, yet roomy enough to accommodate four adults with their oversized luggage (including a hat bag).

It's also probably the only car which actually looked better once covered in stickers. Later in the trip, after driving through puddles of mud, it acquired a new layer of brown which gave it even more kudos. The phrase 'it's not a race it's a rally' took a whole different meaning, as it looked like Tommi Makkinen had escaped a leg of the Rally of Great Britain, and ventured into a five-star hotel.

And last but not least, on the last day, whilst going around the track at the Circuit Paul Ricard, we realised that either most Gumballers had no clue of how to drive their Ferraris and Porsches, or that our car was quite simply vastly superior to theirs.

YORGO MAKES A SPLASH

Frederike Helwig

THE GRAVEL MODE: GO SIDEWAYS!

THE MORE....

YOU TRY....

THE MORE....

YOU'LL LOVE IT!

Feauture Frederike Helwig

This car designed for the video game generation has grip that forgives the most blatant lack of road grip. Use the switch button with options between tarmac, gravel or snow mode. Hit gravel mode, find and empty dust field and you'll feel like Tommi Makkinen. Stay in tarmac mode and watch Ferraris and Porsches vanish in your mirrors.

BOY RACERS

Gumball Factor: ★ ★ ★ ☆ ☆

2002
SUBARU
IMPREZA

WRX STi

If you're looking for a car that will endure the 3,000-mile Gumball Rally, you could do worse than choose one that has won the World Rally Championship. Colin McRae won the world driver's title in 1995 in an Impreza, while Subaru picked up successive manufacturer's titles in 1995, 1996 and 1997. Thanks to this experience in one of the most gruelling types of motor sport, Subaru has a rugged pedigree of robust and reliable cars. The Impreza has built up a phenomenal cult following of road-going speed freaks thanks to its race-ready looks and world-beating reputation. It is an easily available car that instantly lives up to boy racers' expectations, even without modification.

The 2004 Subaru WRX STi featured in the Gumball 3000 is an evolution of the Impreza with increased performance. The intercooled, turbo-charged boxer engine produces 300bhp, while the Electronic Brakeforce Distribution system means each rear wheel can brake independently according to weight transfer and traction. The WRX STi is also all-wheel drive, which is typical of Subaru who pioneered the use of this feature on road vehicles and has since been copied by most major manufacturers.

PERFORMANCE

Max speed:	160 mph
0-60:	4.6 sec
Max power:	333 to the wheels
Miles per gallon:	rousted 18 mpg – 24 cruising
Engine capacity:	2000 cc turbo
Cost when new:	£25.000 + £4000 modifications
Modifications:	New exhaust system, Air filter, fuel pump, better wheels, new suspension and set up, already had fat discs and brembo callipers as standard spec

A good all round contender – it's not a 200 mph + super car but it's got good power, handles well and is pretty much bulletproof when it comes down to reliability. It gave us no problems and I think it looked DOPE!

Text: Tom Trinkle

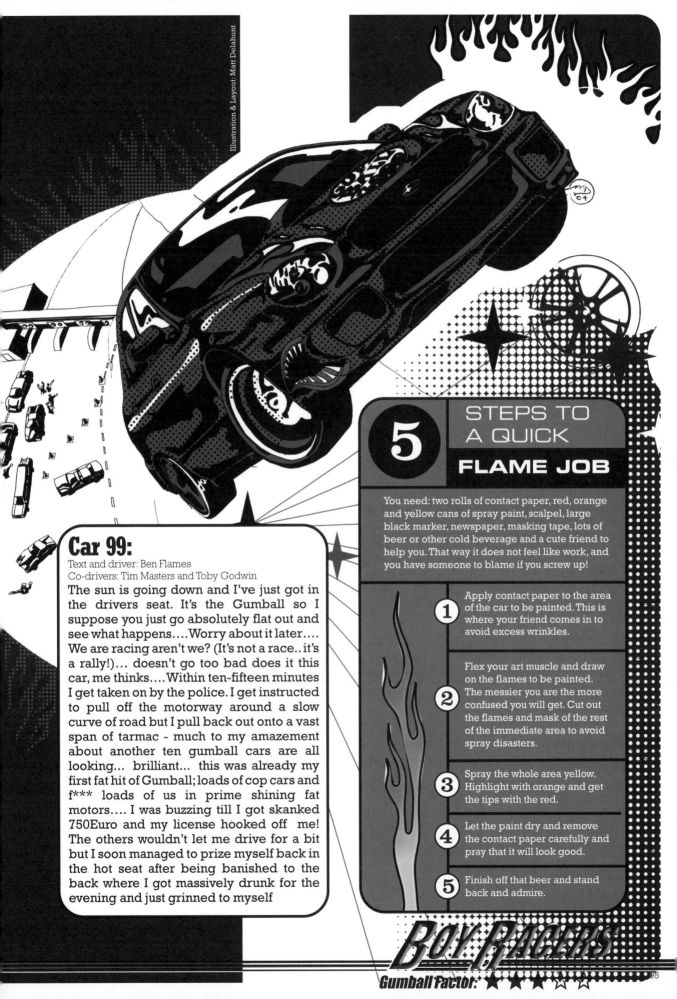

Illustration & Layout: Matt Delahunt

STEPS TO A QUICK FLAME JOB

5

You need: two rolls of contact paper, red, orange and yellow cans of spray paint, scalpel, large black marker, newspaper, masking tape, lots of beer or other cold beverage and a cute friend to help you. That way it does not feel like work, and you have someone to blame if you screw up!

1 Apply contact paper to the area of the car to be painted. This is where your friend comes in to avoid excess wrinkles.

2 Flex your art muscle and draw on the flames to be painted. The messier you are the more confused you will get. Cut out the flames and mask of the rest of the immediate area to avoid spray disasters.

3 Spray the whole area yellow. Highlight with orange and get the tips with the red.

4 Let the paint dry and remove the contact paper carefully and pray that it will look good.

5 Finish off that beer and stand back and admire.

Car 99:

Text and driver: Ben Flames
Co-drivers: Tim Masters and Toby Godwin

The sun is going down and I've just got in the drivers seat. It's the Gumball so I suppose you just go absolutely flat out and see what happens....Worry about it later.... We are racing aren't we? (It's not a race.. it's a rally!)... doesn't go too bad does it this car, me thinks....Within ten-fifteen minutes I get taken on by the police. I get instructed to pull off the motorway around a slow curve of road but I pull back out onto a vast span of tarmac - much to my amazement about another ten gumball cars are all looking... brilliant... this was already my first fat hit of Gumball; loads of cop cars and f*** loads of us in prime shining fat motors.... I was buzzing till I got skanked 750Euro and my license hooked off me! The others wouldn't let me drive for a bit but I soon managed to prize myself back in the hot seat after being banished to the back where I got massively drunk for the evening and just grinned to myself

BOY RACERS

Paul Ricard Circuit

Le BEAUSSET, FRANCE
9th May 2004

Today you get a real chance to drive your cars 'flat out' at the Paul Ricard Formula One Circuit. Lunch will be hosted in the 'Pit Lane' and as a real treat we've organised for all the F1 cars to be on display following yesterdays race!

Fact of the day: Between 1971 and 1990, the Paul Ricard Circuit hosted no fewer than 14 Formula One Grand Prix races!

Hammer

Mileage: **339**

Hours on road: **4-6**

down

Style Tip: Gumball race suits are order of the day!

Sightseeing: Keep a look out for Jenson Button practising how-to-outwit Schuey!

IT'S BOY RACER TIME

Total mileage: **2910**

Situated in the heart of Provence and the vineyards of Bandol, the Paul Ricard High Tech Test Track is 8 km from the medieval village of Le Castellet.

A LEGAL BURST OF CRAZINESS

HOW MUCH TO BUCKINGHAM PALACE?

ANOTHER MINI ADVENTURE!

DYRDEK SECURITY

If you want to stay blingin' on the Gumball, I suggest you bring a security guard. Big Black likes to refer to me as "JACK BAIT".

"We want to go to sleep but we don't. Two little coffees and what are we on? A seven hour trip. Where are we at? Look! Surrounded by hookers... not that I know anything about that."

HALL OF FAME
The Bling Street Skater

Rob Dyrdek

2004 BMW X5

08

DC Shoes had their first experience of the Gumball when Rob took part in 2002 from NY to LA with fellow SEEK skater Josh Kalis in a tuned BMW M5. DC were so suduced by their enthusiasm to go 'Ballin' and by the

Rob Dyrdek

"We don't drive X5's, we give them to our babies' mammas"

Born June 28th 1974, in Dayton Ohio, Rob Dyrdek received a skateb as a Christmas gift in the fall of 1986. Fourteen years later and he international superstar covered in diamonds, transported by fast and protected from persistent fans and hungry media by his loya ever present bodyguard, the mighty 'Big Black'.

Home town: Venice Beach
Career highlights: For a world record I once jumped 17,261 matchbox cars that were on fire!
What's your daily ride? Mercedes CL 500/ U.A.V. / 911 Turbo.
On the rally, you drove a tricked-out 2004 BMW X5 - how tricked-out? I don't know if would consider a stock rental car with one wheel covered in black tape "tricked out"!
I've heard some interesting stories

involving your navigation th Europe... We figured out how t the German navigation system i car without knowing a single wo German. It was without doub biggest mistake. We chose the sh route instead of the quickest. W Paris on a rainy summer afte and by midnight we were in 4 f snow. I was so delirious at one p just thought I drove straig heaven!
Who did most of the driving? pretty much all the driving. Big can barely fit in the Drivers seat X5.
What was your Gumball sound Of course we didn't bring any Thank god someone loaned us Black album. We listened to i and over and over.
What would be your ultimate Gu

"Come over here little donkey, I want you to meet Big Black". Dyrdek and Big Black's compelling raport made them natural stars of the Gumball film '6 Days in May'. Look out for the film and a signature DC Gumball 3000 shoe to be released in the Spring!

Gumball attitude that in 2004 they became Gumball's 'official' Shoe sponsor and decided to send Rob and Big Black to tear up Europe. Only problem was finding a car in Europe big enough to fit Big Black!

Big Black

Christopher "Big Black" Boyken

"We got Welfare cars. You know when they give you a cheque every month"

WATCH AND LEARN BOYS

I would have to say the 911 GT2. ...an come on, that is what LONMAN ...es and he is the King of Gumball. ...re did you find the best skating ...in on the rally? Skating on the ...isn't even possible. I was barely ...cious after all that driving. I ...ly had enough energy to party ...night.

...t was your worst moment on the ...ball? Without a doubt, it would ...to be when we got to Madrid ...driving all night through the ...ntains thinking it was time for ...e much needed sleep. Only to find ...we had another nine hours to ...ella. I was in denial. It took all I ...o not give up after day one.

...t was your best moment on the ...ball? We took all the black tape ...ur car and taped over one side ...snuck through the Spanish road

block. I would also say passing eight cars at a time, including Ferraris and Porsche's, on the dirt shoulder was creating a lot of high fives between me and Big Black in Morroco. Some shit LONMAN would be proud of.

What, to you, is the Spirit of the Gumball? It is more than words can say. I can say what is not the Gumball Spirit, and that is taking your Gumball stickers off your car to avoid a ticket. That is straight Gumball Blasphemy.

Finally, what's the most outrageous thing you've ever done? I bought a bullet proof mask at a spy shop in Paris before the rally. When I got home I let Big Black shoot me in the face with his .22 pistol. Needless to say it broke my jaw in two places.

Please sum up your Gumball 3000 experience in one word?
BALLSTOTHEWALL!!

"He is the best co-pilot. He's so intimdating he can stare cars right out of the way. He is also a solid singer. But you can imagine his 300 plus pounds really limits our top speed."

Home town: Wiggins, MS
Career highlights: Hanging with the Urban Street Donkey in Morocco.
What's your daily ride? Thunderbird LX on DUBS!!! I am an American, I drive American. **Did you have to protect Rob at any point?** Beat anyone up? No but he had to save me a few times from some frisky rich weirdos. **What about when you arrived for breakfast at Real Madrid Stadium? I heard you complaining about the food.** It sucked, they could of at least had some fried chicken up in there. I know they eat chickens in Spain. **How would you have improved the Gumball menu?** I would've put some black cooks up in the kitchen, that's what I would have done. **I heard everywhere you went people thought you were Ruben Studdard from American Idol....** I wish it could have turned into more sexy opportunities for me. I think a lot of these woman missed out on this 300 pounds of lovin. **Who from history would be your dream Gumball co-driver?** Hugh Hefner, cause you know he is gonna have some hot honnies in the car. **What would be your ultimate Gumball car?** Tricked out Winnebago on 24"s! **What's your favorite car related movie?** I would have to go with Kit from 'Knight Rider' cause that was a black car. **What's the most outrageous thing you've ever done?** Falling asleep having a nightmare I was drowning and woke up weeweeing in someone's bed. **Please sum up your Gumball 3000 experience in one word?** Tolerance

HALL OF FAME

The Bodyguard

Christopher 'Big Black'

2004 BMW X5

08

GUMBALL GIRLS

Match the girl to the rumour and win a prize:

1. She's on the Gumball on her honeymoon

2. She's a Japanese movie-star and is supposed to be at her Premiere in Tokyo

3. She can't drive

4. She ended up being the Hottest girl on the rally

5. She's on the gumball to boost her porn career

6. She's a Saudi Princess and bought a Porsche in Paris to do the Gumball with her bodyguard and to annoy her brothers

7. She's a supermodel who met the man of her dreams on the rally and now they're getting married

8. She beat Montoya in a motorbike race

9. She turned up at Gumball HQ the day before the Rally in a

heerleader outfit and
erformed "gimme a G,
gimme a U... etc" to the
mazement of the staff

o. She used to sing with
Michael Jackson in the
ath tub

.1. She used to be a strip-
er

2. She likes dressing up
as a policewoman

3. She's the youngest girl
on the Gumball

4. She's not shy, she can't
speak English

5. They're crew who like
o party

6 She has a butterfly on
er G-string

7. She drives a red Enzo

8. They won the
technomarine
Timekeeping Award

9. She didn't do the really

0. She doesn't shave

1. Her daddy was a race
ar driver

The first 10 correct answers will win 2 tickets to a Kym Mazelle concert!! E-mail your answers to: info@gumball3000.com

G3K CLOTHING

SWEATSHIRT

HOODY

HOODY

GUMBALL 3000
GIVES YOU BALLS

G3K COLLECTION AVAILABLE TO
BUY IN ONLY THE COOLEST STORES
AROUND THE WORLD.

OR FROM OUR WEB SHOP:

WWW.GUMBALL3000.COM

GUMBALL 3000
GIVES YOU BALLS

THE RACE SUIT MAKES YOU FEEL HARD

T-SHIRT

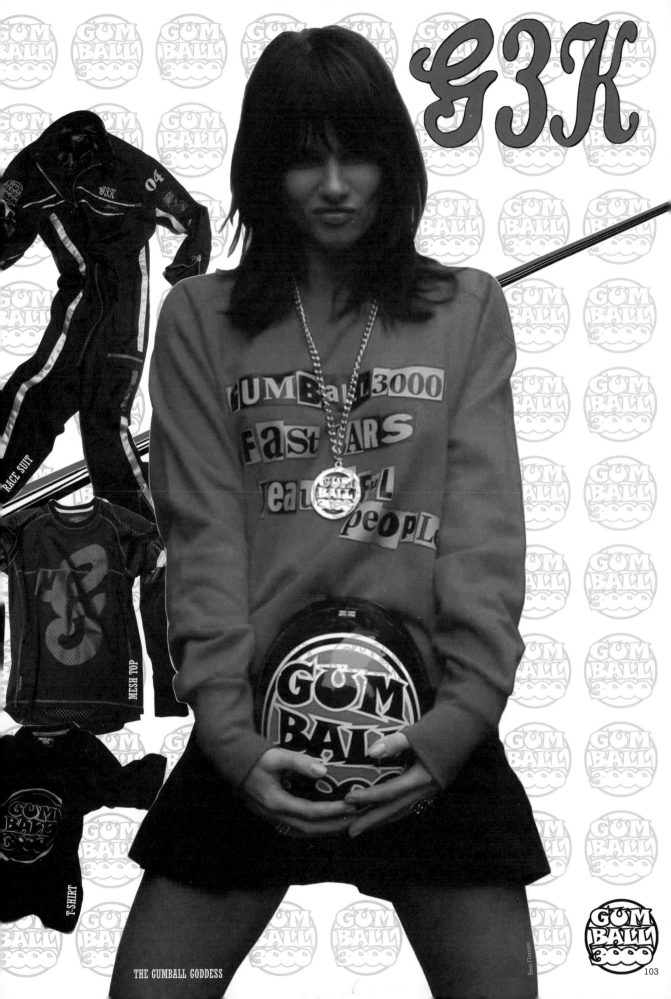

G3K

RACE SUIT

MESH TOP

T-SHIRT

THE GUMBALL GODDESS

Best Flames

GUMBALL GOODIES

AT THE SHARP END OF COOL- THE DAVIDA 'PUDDING' HELMET

TECHNOMARINE DIAMOND-ENCRUSTED LIMITED EDITION WATCH

DAVIDA 'FULL' HELMET

TOP TRUMPS
COLLECTABLE · COMPETITIVE · COMPULSIVE!
SUPERCARS

GUMBALL 3000 SUPERCAR TOP TRUMPS

ALL THE ACTION FROM PREVIOUS GUMBALL'S AVAILABLE ON DVD

IN THE SPIRIT OF TRUE RACING

YOU CANNOT

TAX DISK HOLDER

www.gumball3000.com ®

ASSORTED STICKERS

THE FIRST EVER GUMBALL 3000 ANNUAL

GUMBALL 3000 THE OFFICIAL ANNUAL 2004

BURT REYNOLDS RING SPECIALLY DESIGNED BY HAN CHOLO, COMISSIONED BY GUMBALL 3000

50 CENT HAS ONE OF THESE IN HIS MEDALLION COLLECTION

SUPER QUALITY METAL CAR BADGE SUITABLE FOR YOUR FERRARI OR MINI

LIMITED EDITION BUCKY LASEK GUMBALL 3000 BIRDHOUSE DECK

SOUNDTRACK

BURT REYNOLDS BRONZE BUST, ONLY GIVEN TO GUMBALLERS

SWEAT BANDS & HEADBANDS

Cannes

FINITO!

INTER-CONTINENTAL CARLTON HOTEL, CANNES, FRANCE, 9th May 2004

Take a deep breath, you have just completed 3000 miles in just 6 days, and I hope you've had one of the best adventures of your life!

As you approach Cannes, stay on this beautiful coastal road which becomes the famous Boulevard de La Croisette. Enjoy the drive as you see preparations going on for the Cannes Film Festival that starts tomorrow.

Tonight's party is in the Grand and very famous Ball Room of the Carlton Hotel. So wash, get changed and be ready for dinner, trophies and one major finish party!

Gumball veteran Kim Schmitz, our very own Dr Evil, was the first to arrive in Cannes in his custom Mercedes Benz CL3000 with "Top Secret Gumball Setup!"

How did the car perform? Good enough to win yet another Gumball (note there are no prizes for finishing first, Kim has his own agenda!)

What was your top speed?
175mph.

How much did you spend on fines?
600 Euro for speeding, 350 Euro for participating in an allegedly illegal Race and 500 Euro for bribing cops to stop some competitive Gumballers for 15 minutes!

Did anything break on the car?
Only the members of the media who were crazy enough to drive some of the routes with me!

How much did you spend on fuel?
Nothing. My co-driver from Dubai was the Oil & Fuel expert.

Did you fight with your co-driver?

Yes, after he started driving for 15 minutes and immediately caused a minor accident. After that I drove the entire Gumball myself and he was cheering in the back!

Who would be your dream co-driver?
Mini-Me!

Tell me a little story about your Gumball experience?
The funniest thing was when the Spanish police wanted to put me in prison for 24 hours, for reckless driving. I was holding my breath until I turned red and started shaking a little bit. Then I told the cops that I have diabetes, which was of course a

lie, and I could die if they don't let me buy some medication at the pharmacy. Social engineering at its best.. they released me and my medication was a Whopper from Burger King next to the police station. Five other Gumballers spent the night in prison, wondering how i got away with it, AGAIN... UAHAHAHAHA!!!

What was the best moment on the Gumball?
Arriving first in Cannes!

And your worst moment?
Arriving second in Madrid!

The popularity of Cannes stems from a myriad of things: the location on the sea, the presence of so many powerful Hollywood executives and stars, the legendary tales of sex, topless beaches and debauchery, and the reputation of the festival as a historically significant event in Hollywood's history.

The finish line is reached driving under the Techno-Marine gantry.

In 2004 TechnoMarine became the 'Official Timekeepers' of the event, and entered a specially built Porsche Cayenne Turbo fully kitted out in the company's livery. To commemorate the relationship an innovative 'Limited Edition' Gumball 3000 watch has been created with a bezel set with 135 full cut white diamonds. A limited edition of just 3000 of these exclusive watches will be hand crafted signifying the total number of miles that the rally covers, and each will be uniquely numbered. A must have for all die hard watch collectors and Gumball fans alike!

Style Tip: Hollywood stars from Charlize Theron to Brad Pitt guarantee glamour on the red carpet later in the week, but they will have to share the spotlight with the Gumball army of 'beautiful people!' Though this is perhaps not the place to wear your new galabiyya, slippers and Fez!

Sightseeing: Look out for old women walking tiny dogs. Beautiful women walking tiny dogs, and tiny dogs walking women!

Main photo: Fiona McLaren. Collage photos: Fly James McNaught, Gray and Tom. AC/K Boyd, Jeaton.

esented by the Mayor of Cannes
he Special Cannes Palm D'or Award goes to...

The 6th Annua

The Bentley Boys

Ian Quest, Kevin Jones, Adrian Butler and Richard Harrison in their 1986 Union Jack painted Bentley for sheer quintessential British style.

he EA Games "award goes to...

Supermodel Jodie Kidd and Joe Macari in their 2004 Maserati Coupe; and Robert Bowen-West and Maurizio Fabris in their 2004 Porsche 996 GT3 RS

"Need for Speed"

ilver Han Cholo Designed Bling Rings' go to...

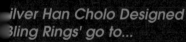

ALL PARTICIPANTS RECIEVED A SOLID BUST OF THEIR HERO BURT REYN APPROPRIATELY WEARING A FEZ FOR ME ACHIEVING THE ENDURANCE.

The Ambassadors

Mourad 'Momo' Mazouz and Ramdane Touhami driving a 2001 Bentley Continental R were awarded "Ambassadors of the Gumball' for their kind introduction to the King of Morocco. The King welcomed the Gumball with open arms, organising police escorts and support throughout the whole country. Without their help many of us would still be lost in Morocco somewhere.

Gumball 3000
Awards

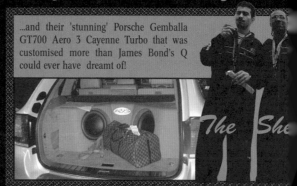

...and their 'stunning' Porsche Gemballa GT700 Aero 3 Cayenne Turbo that was customised more than James Bond's Q could ever have dreamt of!

The She...

...BALL ORGANISERS MAXIMIILLION AND JULIE PRESENTING AWARDS IN THE FAMOUS CARLTON HOTEL BALLROOM

Technomarine Timekeeping awa...

Allison Cornia and Cassandra Dungan in a 2003 Porsche 996 for always arriving stylishly on time.

Allison and Cassa...

The Style Award goes to...

Last year's Spirit of the Gumball winner Alexander Roy and Amanda Kinsley for their outragous antics disguised as Royal Canadian Mountain Police, Swedish Highway Patrol, German Polizei and Tron. They used the sirens on their 2001 BMW M5 to pull over unsuspecting Gumballers.

The Undercover Cops

And the 'Spirit of the Gum...

Winners of the

SPIRIT of the GUMBALL

Text: Julia Martens

LJ: I saw you guys squeeze right past the long line of Gumball cars on the main sea front road waiting to park!

John: Yeah, they all went 'I can't believe you guys did it in 20 minutes we've been waiting here for an hour and forty minutes. And we were like, "Ok – see ya!"

Gary: Yeah and at the front of the hotel there was about 6 VIP parking spaces. And they moved a Lamborghini out of the way to make room for us…. Hahahaha!

John: It was mad.. we gave announcement of our arrival with our musical airhorn non-stop, and we had boom mikes coming though the open roof!

Congratulations for winning the Spirit of the Gumball award! So, er.. what is the spirit..?

Gary: It was tears, laughter….

John: We just GOT there. We had a couple of breakdowns but nothing major and we just finished it. Bearing in mind that our top speed was a third of everyone else's, we averaged 60 and everyone else 180. We're here at the finish line in Cannes along with everyone else.

LJ: What was your maximum speed?

Gary: Cruising speed was 65, max speed at a push was 70. We had it to 85 once going down hill and the wind blowing in our direction!

LJ: So did you even make it to any check points or parties?

John: 2 or 3, Barcelona was the only hotel we made it to in daylight.

TRUE GUMBALL SPIRIT

Gary Lutke

Gary: But we had a good party in Barcelona. We went into the city centre with a couple guys to hit some nightclubs but Barcelona on a Sunday night is pretty quiet. So we found this one place open but they were charging 50 Euro a head, and we weren't having any of that so we told them that this older guy we were with, Allen, was Michael Schumachers head of security.

John: We told them he's been looking after Schumacher all weekend for the grand prix. and since Schumacher has jut gone to bed he's now allowed out for a beer…

Gary: So they let us in and the word spread

that he was Michael Schumacher's head of security so everyone was coming in to talk to us in the night club. It was a great way to talk to girls! Hahaha!

LJ: Surely you had no problems talking to girls, come on… a 2CV? Any other style tips?

Gary: Hmmmm…..We had 3 t-shirts between the two of us. To clean ourselves up upon arrival at check points we turned our t-shirts inside out. Same with our pants really. Haha!

John: Obviously we didn't have much space because we had the rollcage in the back – two spare wheels, spare parts, so we couldn't actually take that much luggage. We had the two Gumball t-shirts that we wore. We just kept on running out of clothes and eventually we just had to go commando.

LJ: hmmm.. best moment on the Gumball?

Illustration: Luc Janin

HERBIE MOVE OVER

Gary: We were 3-4 hours out of the first check point at Mas du Clos in the middle of France and we were running on an empty tank….

John: We'd already given our two spare 20 litre fuel cans to other Gumballers who'd run out of petrol on the way out of Paris.

Gary: So we coasted it down this hill and came to a stop at this petrol station which wasn't due to open for another 6 hours and so we resigned to sit there. We thought the game was up really, because we would loose so much time, but then out of nowhere on this dark desolate French country road, another Citroen 2CV turned up!

John: It turned out to be a mad French guy, a local restaurant owner on his way home from work. He saw us in the forecourt and turned his car around. His English was as good as our French but he looked into our car, pulled the fuel cans out and took us to another petrol station which was open that only someone who lived in the town would know about. And within half an hour we were back on the road again and on our way… it was good karma.

LJ: Worst moment?

John: When we broke down in Morocco, right on the edge of the dessert at 10 o'clock at night.

LJ: were there any tears?

John: Nearly. I mean breaking down in that part of the world at that time of night… But what had happened was that the spark plug had unscrewed itself and popped out and so we screwed it back in again and off we went!

Gary: The car is a bit like a Meccano set. It comes off and you just screw it back on.

LJ: So what's the driver's report?

John: Over all the car was comfortable…

Gary: …except, the way the engine was made, and the way we had it modified, it got really hot and the heat came through the bulkhead into the footwell and so our feet just got roasted… and so did the hi-fi, so we could only listen to two cds at a go and then we had to switch it off for 2 hours before we could switch it back on.

John: It got us home and it never started the following morning!

LJ: And would you do it again?

Gary: Definitely. But we are looking into doing it in something a little bit faster next year. We are possibly looking into an ice-cream van…. That would be quite god fun.

Hyper Cool

Allez!

tiggrrrrrr ...

112

Meguia's

TechnoMarine

FECK ME I'M FAMOUS! FECK ME I'M FAMOUS!

Dan Anslow

Ubu

1990 2CV

Oh la la

⁴ Wheels under an Umbrella

Meguiar's

FECK ME

THE GENERAL LEE IS REBORN

PERFORMANCE

Text & Driver: Gary Lutke & John Docherty

Max speed(mph):	Cruising speed 65, max speed at a push was 70. 85 once going down hill and the wind blowing in our direction
0-60:	20 seconds!!!
Max power:	30 DIN bhp @ 5750rpm, 39 Nm @ 3500rpm
Miles per gallon:	42 to 50 mpg
Engine capacity:	602 cc air-cooled flat twin
Cost when new:	$900
Total produced:	3 872 583
Modifications:	Racing coils, Heads skimmed, Carburettor rebuild, Roll cage, Racing suspension and de-chocked, Orange paint job, Rebel flag roof, Dixie airhorns, full homage to the Dukes of Hazard, a stereo and a digital clock

Commonly nicknamed the 'ugly duck' by the Dutch, the 'lame duck' by the Germans and the 'tin snail' by the English, this French design classic has met with its fair share of scorn. When the 2CV was unveiled in Paris in 1948, journalists sneered at its radical design, but it went on to prove very popular and stayed in production till 1990. The name 2CV is an abbreviation of 'deux cheveaux' (French for 'two horses') after its tax horsepower rating.

When designer Pierre Boulanger began work on the car in the 1930's he was trying to fulfil an unusual brief. He wanted to make an affordable 'umbrella on four wheels' that two peasants could drive 100kg of farm produce to market at a speed of 60kmh across muddy tracks if necessary. The brief also specified that the car must use no more than three litres of petrol to travel 100km and that the suspension would offer a smooth enough ride that the 2CV could carry a cargo of eggs across a ploughed field without breaking them. It wasn't until after World War Two that Boulanger's design became a reality (Citroen hid the project during the war for fear it might be used by the Germans for military applications) and he had created a classic whose unique shape, reliability and low running costs would attract a worldwide following.

A 2CV famously appeared in the 1981 James Bond film For Your Eyes Only, after which Citroen offered a limited edition '2CV James Bond' model to the consumer market featuring a yellow paintjob, '007' emblazoned on the doors and fake bullet holes peppering the bodywork. A 2CV also appears briefly in the famous Air Cavalry scene of Apocalypse Now; only briefly because it is blown to shreds by a rocket as it crosses a bridge!

ECCENTRICS

مراكش الجديدة الرباط*   **مطار محمد الخامس

* THE SACRED TALKING 'BURT REYNOLDS' STATUE IS IN GREAT DANGER. THOSE CRAZY GUMBALLERS HAVE MISTAKEN IT FOR ONE OF THEIR TROPHIES. DR EVIL HAS HEARD OF ITS' GREAT POWER AND WILL DO ANYTHING TO GET HIS HANDS ON IT.
** HE WILL USE IT TO TAKE OVER THE WORLD! BURT HELP US! ...FIVE OR SIX SUGAR?

OUR STORY BEGINS IN PARIS...

WELCOME BACK RACE FANS! AMONG THE ENTRANTS AT THIS YEAR'S GUMBALL 3000, WE HAVE: BUNNY, MAX MILLIONS, THE NOTORIOUS DR EVIL, SOME DODGY EAST END WHEELER DEALER, EXTREME SK8TERBOY BADAZZIO... AND OF COURSE, THE LEGENDARY CAPTAIN GUMBALL!!!

...AND THE FLAG DROPS! MAX MILLIONS BOUGHT THE LEAD!

A FEW DAYS LATER, SOMEWHERE IN MOROCCO.

IT IS COMPLETE CHAOS LADIES AND GENTLEMEN...

HMM... DOCTOR EVIL... HE MUST HAVE ESCAPED FROM PRISON. BUT WHAT IS HE DOING HERE?

HEY, CAPTAIN NO BALLS... WILL YOU BE OK TO FOLLOW?

THE GUMBALLERS HAVE ALL MYSTERIOUSLY SLEPT IN AND HAVE TO CATCH THE BOAT BACK TO EUROPE BY SUNSET!

BUT THAT'S JUST THE START OF THEIR TROUBLES... A COLLAPSED BRIDGE IS NOW BLOCKING THEIR ROUTE TO THE PORT.

HEY, CAP GB DUDE   WHAT'RE WE GONNA DO?

I KNEW DR EVIL WAS UP TO NO GOOD.

JUST THEN, A MYSTERIOUS SMOKING ROLLS-ROYCE PULLS UP TO CAPTAIN GUMBALL...

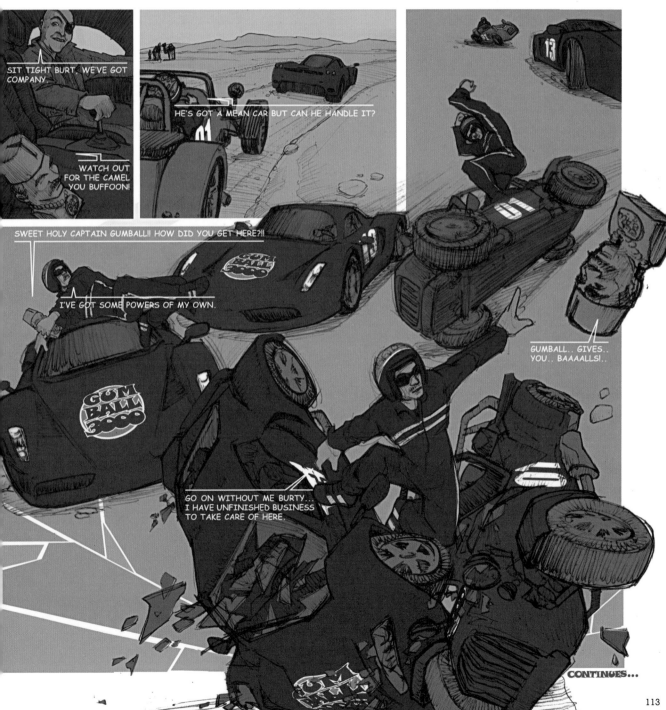

113

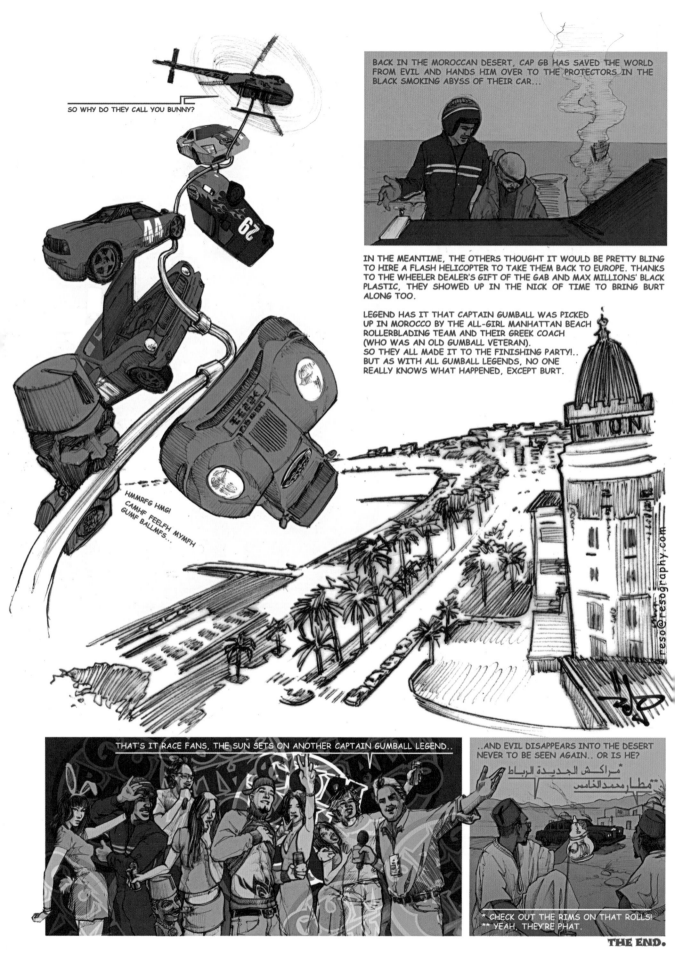

SO WHY DO THEY CALL YOU BUNNY?

BACK IN THE MOROCCAN DESERT, CAP GB HAS SAVED THE WORLD FROM EVIL AND HANDS HIM OVER TO THE PROTECTORS IN THE BLACK SMOKING ABYSS OF THEIR CAR...

IN THE MEANTIME, THE OTHERS THOUGHT IT WOULD BE PRETTY BLING TO HIRE A FLASH HELICOPTER TO TAKE THEM BACK TO EUROPE. THANKS TO THE WHEELER DEALER'S GIFT OF THE GAB AND MAX MILLIONS' BLACK PLASTIC, THEY SHOWED UP IN THE NICK OF TIME TO BRING BURT ALONG TOO.

LEGEND HAS IT THAT CAPTAIN GUMBALL WAS PICKED UP IN MOROCCO BY THE ALL-GIRL MANHATTAN BEACH ROLLERBLADING TEAM AND THEIR GREEK COACH (WHO WAS AN OLD GUMBALL VETERAN). SO THEY ALL MADE IT TO THE FINISHING PARTY!.. BUT AS WITH ALL GUMBALL LEGENDS, NO ONE REALLY KNOWS WHAT HAPPENED, EXCEPT BURT.

HMMRFG HMG! CAMHF FEELFH MYMFH GUMF BALLMFS...

LYON

reso@resography.com

THAT'S IT RACE FANS, THE SUN SETS ON ANOTHER CAPTAIN GUMBALL LEGEND..

..AND EVIL DISAPPEARS INTO THE DESERT NEVER TO BE SEEN AGAIN.. OR IS HE?

*مراكش الجديدة الرباط
**مطار محمد الخامس

* CHECK OUT THE RIMS ON THAT ROLLS!
** YEAH, THEY'RE PHAT.

THE END.

114

DRIVING INNOVATION
Smart Thinking

PERFORMANCE
Text & Driver: Stephen & Brian Elford

Max speed:	110 mph
0-60:	12 secs
Max power:	96 bhp at wheel
Miles per gallon:	43 mpg
Engine capacity:	700cc
	Turbocharged
Cost when new:	$12,000
Total produced:	350k so far

Modifications: Front and rear suspension springs up rated and lowered 25mm, larger vented and drilled discs fitted to front with competition pads, engine remapped, induction scope, K&N filter, stainless steel performance exhaust, dump valve, blue neon under lights!

The car was not a speed machine on the open roads but when we got to Morocco it came into its own. The narrow, tight, twisting roads and the car came alive. The handling enabled me to overtake some of the others in their Porsche's, Ferrari's etc. Many of the others at the checkpoints were amazed at "that pesky Smart car, I can't get it out of my rear view mirror!" It might not have been fast but it cornered like it was on rails!!!

Novel, and truly classless, in a way that the original Mini was and the new MINI will never be. Rich people own them, poorer people own them, and the rest point and smile from the bus.

Smart car
2003 city coupe

Since it was first launched in 2000, the dinky Smart car has gained quite a following among trendy city dwellers around the world and now it has become the smallest car ever to compete in the Gumball Rally. The Smart City Coupe engineered by Daimler Chrysler not only stands out in a crowd, its design is entirely suited to urban driving. For example, its small dimensions mean it is as long as some 'normal' cars are wide, allowing the Smart to park 'end-on'. In addition, the emission levels are very low, so low in fact the car is even exempt from tax in Germany where there are tight regulations on emissions. Power from the Smart's three cylinder turbo-charged petrol engine is transmitted to the rear wheels, while the front wheels are fitted with narrow tyres to help prevent the car from rolling over.

I was raising funds for the Diana, Princess of Wales Children's Hospital in Birmingham. The hospital is a self funded charity that treats over 300,000 young patients a year. It is renowned throughout the world for it's treatment of some of the rarest, most complex and life threatening conditions found in children, and has offered treatment to the war torn regions of Europe and the Middle East.

Just over two years ago a very close friend's daughter was diagnosed with Leukemia. The hospital kept her spirit high - thanks to all the hard work and dedication from the staff. At the end of November last year the leukemia had gone into remission.

We only rent our time on this planet - Make the most of every minute.
Text: Stephen Elford

The novel shape of this titchy two-seater incorporates a TRIDION safety shell made of reinforced steel as well as replaceable multi-coloured plastic panels that can be changed according to the owner's taste within an hour. On the inside, the styling is how a child might imagine a futuristic car's interior to look, with rotating pods and rounded shapes. The Smart has been the first truly tiny city car to achieve notoriety and an appearance in the Gumball will certainly add to its reputation. By the way, if you had any doubts about this odd buggy, British racing legend Stirling Moss drives one – what higher recommendation could you get?

CHRIS EUBANK HITCHES A RIDE - VERY SMART

ECCENTRICS

A Gumball veteran, Richie Rich first took part in the 2000 rally around europe in his matt black 1970 Dodge Challenger complete with the World's 'largest sound system'. Unfortunately the Dodge lost its gearbox mid-rally, although he made up for the loss by sharing a rental car to reach the finish line with British 'it girl' Tara Palmer Tomkinson (who had blown a tire on her Jaguar)! The following year, this time in his 8-series (minus flame-throwers), Richie can be seen chauffeuring the exhausted Johnny Knoxville in the famed Gumball episode of Jackass! This time he was back to give Gumball more abuse, flame throwers and all!

"I MUST REMEMBER TO PUT IN OIL!" (2000)

"I MUST REMEMBER TO PUT IN OIL!" (2004)

WE'RE THE GUMBALL ANTICHRISTS

ALL DRIVERS AND PASSENGERS ARE FROM ESSEX OR BLONDE!! →

UGLY BASTARD BEHIND WHEEL - RICH

RICHIE WARREN IS THE DRIVER

DAN ANSLOW IS THE PASSENGER

BEN ROUSSEAU IS TOO BIG TO BE IN THE BACK SEAT BUT WE BROUGHT HIM ANY WAY

The car itself is from the Fuel stable. All of Fuel's cars are matt black and we now have a collective of Fuel fans across the UK who are painting their cars matt black too. It's seen as two fingers up to the shiny, polished car scene – paint your car black, get rockets on it, sirens, nitrous, whatever – and get out there and go crazy!

"We have a belief that if you are going to do the Gumball you have to create a vehicle that is wild, crazy, and very wacky races. If you turn up with a silver Porsche, stick some stickers on and think you're in for a rich boys knees-up then we will be gunning for you!"

AND HAVE BEEN SENT TO MAKE THIS A
ROAD FROM HELL

IF IT'S TOO LOUD, YOU'RE TOO OLD

Fuel started as a record label making music specifically for sound systems – intelligent, bass heavy music in surround sound. We built two sound system cars from two 1970 Dodge Challengers (matt black of course) – they have six 18" subs in the back of each, and mids and tops that rise out of the boot on hydraulics – we took them to Daytona where they won the title of loudest cars in the world. They became the left and right speaker, creating one mother of a car sound system! We took them to the V festival and they were so loud you couldn't hear the Prodigy on stage - their sound guys came over and begged us to turn them off!

Fuel team used their sirens to pull over er Gumballers on the road before speeding t, blasting the flame thrower and firing

rockets out the roof at them. The plan backfires when they stop a red Porsche in Morocco to borrow money to pay off the local mafia – only

to discover it is a car they nearly destroyed back in Spain.....

"IT HAS A VERY SPECIAL MAGNETIC APPEAL FOR BABES WITH A REAL TWISTED APPRECIATION OF THE DARK SIDE."

"IS THIS WHERE THE OIL GOES?"

"CAN ANYONE SMELL BURNING?"

ile rushing to catch the Ferry in Nador they a puncture on one of the low-profile tyres. Gumballer with a BMW M5 lends his spare

wheel, which is half as wide but vaguely as big. It rubs against the wheel arch so Dan and Ben have to lean out the window for the next 150

miles catamaran-style. Our hitchkiker Julia Joy gets in the lush car behind and watches a movie instead!

69TH PRECINCT

PERFORMANCE
1991 BMW 850i

Max Speed:	180mph
0-60:	5.3 secs
Max power:	550 bhp
Miles per gallon:	8
Engine capacity:	6.0 litre
Cost when new:	$85,000
Total produced:	1,500

MODIFICATIONS:

We've had a massive installation of X-Boxes, screens and sound systems put in. The car does its tour of duty when it's not in the Gumball. X-Box hosts the Street Car Challenge inside the car.

Wide arch body kit by Zeemax
Wheels by Rial (Rial Daytona's) supplied by Wolfrace
Tyres by Yokohama
Sound system Vibe Audio
Screens and head unit Clarion
X-Box crystal by Microsoft
Police sirens and lights by Met Police
Flame throwers are Lpg direct gas injection fitted and supplied by Nitrous Power (Huntingdon)
Engine work carried out by Xtreme Autos Ireland and is top secret

I'M A FIRE STARTER, TWISTED FIRE STARTER

ECCENTRICS

DJ royalty

Good times with Norman jay mbe

"COME ON NORMAN CRANK IT UP!"

A self confessed 'beatle baby' born in Notting Hill, London, of West Indian parents, the young Jay had unwittingly displayed latent dj'ing talents even from the tender age of eight. These talents received a fitting tribute nearly three decades later, when in June 2002 he was officially cited in the Queen's Diamond Jubilee Honours list to be appointed a Member of the Order of the British Empire, an MBE no less!

He is arguably one of the finest and most respected dj's in the world today whose talents and many years of dedicated service to his profession have now seen him rightfully acknowledged by the highest authority in the land. He has played for the likes of Mick Jagger at his exclusive 50th birthday party - Robert Di Nero, Michael Caine, George Michael, Will Smith, Prince, Bruce Springsteen, and Jamiroquai, who affectionately calls him the 'Godfather'.

You choose your gigs on the basis of 'People and places'. Why this one? I'd heard about the Gumball and felt honoured to do the closing party in Cannes. I knew it would be somewhere people probably hadn't heard of me. People all with different backgrounds to my own-it would be a meeting of two different worlds.

It was the A-Z of people, and I loved the camaraderie! What united these people was a shared love of adventure and cars.

That's what I enjoy. The excitement in the process of discovery.

Did it live up to your expectations? It was better than the hype. It's the people. The enthusiasm. The dashing daring of this disparate group of people. To make them all dance in one place. Some had just arrived in town after this race and were exhausted and should have gone to bed, but instead they're straight in there dancing. Going 'Come on Norman Crank it up!' That was amazing energy.

What kind of set did you play? Good-time funky party set. The majority of people don't come from clubbing and music background. But they are all people who live life to the full – live hard, play hard, party hard. I give them a set that reflects that. It's all about enjoying yourself. It's all about expression. Self-expression.

Talking cars now - what's your daily ride? Mini Cooper original shape.

Any Modifications? It's an old model so I needed to modify it – central locking, automatic windows,wooden dash, leather interior!

Sound system? I'm not a fan of ice in cars - ice in clubs and at home. Music in cars is too boyracerish for me!

Did you check out the cars as they drove through the finish line? Saw more Porsche's and Lambo's than one could shake a stick at. I've never seen such an assemble of high performance cars in one race, in the same place.

Since we're in Cannes for the film festival, what's your favorite car related movie? Obviously has to be the one that turned me onto Minis in the first place. The original Italian Job. I saw that and just thought, 'must have, must get!' Since then I've always owned a mini. Even when I was driving other cars. It's a love affair!

I've had a '69 original mark 2 with 10 inch wheels that got stolen. Last year I bought a late special edition Cooper 1.3, last one before new BMW shape. Night-fire red.

I've had 10-12 in my time, some lasted weeks, some months. They were cheap you know, and when you don't have any money. I would buy them for spare parts and take bits trying to keep one on the road.

If you were to do the Gumball what would be your ultimate Gumball car? (Without hesitation) A mini. (After a little thought) A Cooper S mark 1-3. Late model, multi-point injection Cooper, or if I could get one similar I'd work it. I'm more into the original ethos of the Gumball. The fun ride and people element- like the 2 CV- I'd be more at the back end. You need a serious mark to be at the front end!

I'd love to do it in a mini if someone would donate one. (Sponsors take note!!)

Who would you bring as your co-pilot? Anyone who'd wanna risk their lives driving with me. I'd want to be part of a team of us doing it. Preferably someone beautiful. (Beauties take note!!)

What would be your soundtrack? Something cruis-y. Soulful jazzy funky dancy. Night driving cruisy. Music that gives you a sense of freedom

Most interesting car-related experience? Surviving in a fatal crash. Getting up and walking away.

So what was your overall impression of this group of people who had just lapped a 3000 mile circuit around Europe and Africa? What was the atmosphere like from the DJ booth? Loved it because for me it was a true to life, 3-dimensional version of wacky races. A living breathing one, a real Penelope Pitstop. All those characters were in there in the flesh. It was a cartoon come to life.

There wasn't a DJ in the original [Cannonball Run] series so I don't know where I come in. But I'm glad they did get a DJ in this time around.

Illustrations and layout by Matt Delahunt

Adrien Brody
(Oscar Winner)

Big Black
(Dyrdek Security)

Cuban Brothers

Rob Dyrdek (Pro-Skater)

Rachel Hunter
(Supermodel)

Carey Hart
(FMX Champion)

Damon Hill
(Ex F1 World Champion)

Bruce Reynolds
(Great Train Robber)

Nick Moran (Actor)

Bez (Happy Mondays)

Goldie (DJ)

Sal (US Sports Presente

Kym Mazelle
(Soul Diva)

Travis Pastrana
(MX Legend)

Pam Hogg
(Punk Fashion Icon)

Tara Dakides
(Snowboarding Champion)

Shane (The Legend)

Playmates of the Year

Julian Lennon
(Son of John)

Bam Margera
(Jackass, Pro-Skater)

Ron Jeremy (Porn Star)
Jodie Marsh (Model)

Vince Neal (Motley Crue)

Norman Jay MBE (DJ)

Jenson Button (F1 Driver)

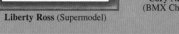

Liberty Ross (Supermodel)

Cory Nastazio
(BMX Champion)

RS 1. Chris Eubank 2. Sean Ryder 3. Bruce Reynolds 4. Bez 5. Johnny Knoxville 6. Chris Pontius 7. Steve O 8. Maximillion
s Pastrana 10. Carey Hart 11.Tara Palmer-Tomkinson 12. Ryan Dunn 13. Jodie Kidd 14. Tony Hawk 15. Rob Dyrdek 16. Big Black 17. Adrien Brody 18. Bucky Lasek 19.Shane Slevin

MUMMY BEATS MONTOYA

Hey, this is fun! I'm getting the hang of it!

What are they trying to do. Kill each other!

I've got you on this corner

Don't even think about it Juan Pablo. I've got the racing line!

Wow, she's pretty good at this, and this is supposed to be her first time?

HALL OF FAME

...Mar Superstar
(Singer)

Burt Reynolds
(Actor)

Johnny Knoxville
(Jackass)

Joel Madden
(Good Charlotte)

Dannii Minogue
(Popstar)

...rnesto Viso
(...00 Champion)

Chris Eubank
(Ex Boxing Champion)

Hugh Hefner
(Playboy)

Tara Palmer-Tomkinson
(IT Girl)

Chris Pontius (Jackass)

Bucky Lasek (Pro-Skater)

...ve 0 (Jackass)

Lady Victoria Hervey

Ryan Dunn (Jackass)

Jodie Kidd (Supermodel)

Tyler Evans
(MX Champion)

...Hawk (Pro-Skater)

Jesse James
(West Coast Choppers)

Ruby Wax (TV Presenter)

Jason Priestley (Actor)
Maximillion (Gumball Boss)

Vic Reeves
(Comedian)

1. "I'm a Gumballer man. Through and through" 2. "Poor old Nuts had his 'blue' hair turned grey after going on the Gumball rally" 3. "The Gumball is one of the last great adventures" 4. "I went to check the rear view mirror an' saw a Lamborghini and the $1,000,000 McLaren F1 tearin' up behind me. Seconds later I was left eatin' the dust" 5. "If you've seen the Burt Reynolds film called 'The Cannonball Run', its kinda' like that" 6. "The Russian police, stern, stern but fair" 7. "It's aristocratic delinquency. You cannot rage harder than Gumball. So awesome" 8. "From a business point of view, I'd say I've definitely been inspired by Richard Branson" 9. "Gumball is the greatest race I have ever been able to attend – can't wait for next year" 10. "I had a blast!" 11. "That was the best 7 days I have ever, ever had!" 12. "Lets all get drunk and f**k each other" 13. "They were getting a little bit overexcited seeing a blonde girl driving a Dodge Viper" 14. "I tested the car's top speed at one point because...well, I had to" 15. "We don't drive X5's, we give them to our babies Mamas!" 16. "We got a welfare car. You know when they give you a cheque every month!" 17. "My Moroccan Oscar!" 18. "Have you ever heard of a vacation from a vacation? That's what you'll need after Gumball 3000" 19. "I haven't washed my dick in 6 days"

...Maximillion and Julie were guests at the French Grand Prix Circuit at Magny Cours. Alpine Stars hosted a 'mini motorbike' race with their ...Formula One sponsored drivers and they invited 'Gumball' to take part. To Max's reluctance, Julie decides she wants have a go. Undeterred by ...he professional grid of riders including Formula One's star drivers Juan Pablo Montoya and Kimi Raikkonen she swaps her Jimmy Choos ...or a pair of Alpine Stars boots and sits on the start line. After she asks the questions "which lever do I pull" and "how do I stop", a lot of ...worried faces started to imagine an accident in the making. "These bikes do over 50mph" the Alpine Stars representative told her, trying ...o put her off having a go. After a very sketchy warm up lap the chequered flag drops, and the rest as they say is pure Gumball history.....

...e on Mummy!

Hi Lotus, Mummy will be finished in a minute

Wow, my Mummy is beating Formula One Champion Juan Pablo Montoya??!

WOW! That chick with the diamonds WON!

Damn, I've never been beaten by a girl. I'll never live this down with the other drivers!

That was easy. I think I'll try Formula One next week. Hey Ron, have you got a seat available?